TYEE COOKBOOK

By
Dorothy Harshman, Carol James and Rena Lude

Edited by
Mereda Metz and Rosemary Easter

The **Tyee Cookbook** has been published as a cooperative venture between the University of Washington Athletic Department and the University of Washington Alumni Association.

Peanut Butter Publishing
Seattle

Cover design: Neil Sweeney
Cover photo: Tom Moore
Illustrations: Roger Thias
Book design: Victoria Hagar & Neil Sweeney
Typestyle: Italia, set by Tom Marshall & Dianne Taugher
Table setting provided by Consolidated Restaurants

ISBN 0–89716–102–5

CONTENTS

Acknowledgments

A cookbook doesn't just appear. Like a good meal it is developed, course by course, page by page. This book wouldn't have become a reality without the help of numerous "cooks."

The main course was provided by Mereda Metz, who brought the idea to the Athletic Department. Without her initiative and energy there would not be a Tyee Cookbook. The second largest helping was provided by Rosemary Easter, who volunteered to work with Mereda and soon joined her as co-editor.

Help came from many other areas as well. Our thanks go to the Tyees, the University of Washington faculty and staff, and the Husky athletes who provided their recipes.

Working behind the scenes in the Athletic Department were Ruth Joseph, Jeanne Grainger, Lugene St. Cyr, Barbara Grund, Kathy Gerken, Pat Wilson, Suzanne Crawford and Karen Rosenzweig. Tracy King, director of the Alumni Association, also volunteered his office's help, and, as is his custom, asked nothing in return.

A special thanks to Elliott Wolf, owner of Peanut Butter Publishing, who willingly offered advice and suggestions long before he was selected to be the book's publisher.

Without these and many other people's assistance, the publication of this book would have been impossible.

Dorothy Harshman,
Carol James,
Rena Lude

APPETIZERS

Chicken Teriyaki

1 dozen chicken wings
¼ c soy sauce
¼ c lemon juice

1 clove garlic, crushed
2 tbsp sugar
1 tsp grated fresh ginger

Cut the wings in half and remove the tips. Combine the remaining ingredients and pour the mixture over the chicken in a shallow pan. Marinate at room temperature for at least 1 hour or overnight in the refrigerator. Remove the wings from the marinade and broil for 20–30 minutes, basting them frequently with marinade and turning once.

Makes 24.

Dennis Brown,
Athlete

Mousse de Foies de Volaille

Chicken liver mousse

1 lb or 2 c chicken livers
2 tbsp minced shallots
2 tbsp butter
⅓ c Madeira or Cognac
½ tsp salt

¼ c whipping cream
⅛ tsp allspice
⅛ tsp pepper
Pinch of thyme
½ c butter, melted

Clean the livers and remove any attached bits of membrane. Cut them into ½" pieces. Sauté the livers with the shallots for 2–3 minutes, until the livers are just stiffened, but still rosy inside. Place in a blender jar. Pour the wine or Cognac into the sauté pan and boil it rapidly until it has reduced to 3 tbsp. Add it to the blender jar, then pour in the cream and seasonings. Cover and blend at top speed for several seconds until the liver is a smooth paste. Add the melted butter and blend for several seconds more. Force the mixture through a fine-meshed sieve, then check seasonings. Pack into a jar, cover and chill for at least 2–3 hours.

Makes 2½ c.

Julianne (Mrs. James) Collier,
Tyee

Super Nachos

½ lb lean ground beef
½ lb chorizo sausage, casing
  removed
1 large onion, chopped
Salt
Liquid hot pepper seasoning
1 or 2 (1-lb) cans refried beans
1 (4-oz) can whole California
  green chiles, chopped

2–3 c grated Monterey Jack
  or mild Cheddar cheese
¾ c prepared taco sauce
  (green or red)
Garnishes (suggestions
  below)
8 c crisp-fried tortilla
  pieces or corn-flavored
  chips

Crumble the ground beef and sausage in a frying pan. Add the onion and cook on high heat, stirring until the meat is lightly browned. Drain any excess fat and season with salt and liquid hot pepper seasoning to taste. Spread the beans in a shallow 10" x 15" pan or an overproof dish. Spread evenly with the meat, then sprinkle the chiles over the bean/meat mixture and cover with the cheese. Drizzle the taco sauce over the top. Cover and chill if made ahead. Bake, uncovered, in a 400° oven for 20–25 minutes or until very hot throughout. Remove from the oven and quickly garnish with some or all of the following: about ¼ c chopped green onion and about 1 c pitted ripe olives; in the center, mound 1 (8-oz) can avocado dip or 1 medium-size ripe avocado, peeled, pitted and coarsely mashed and top with about 1 c sour cream; a mild red pickled pepper and fresh coriander or parsley sprigs. Quickly tuck the fried tortilla pieces or corn-flavored chips just around the edges of the bean mixture, making a petaled flower effect and serve at once. Keep the nachos hot on an electric warming tray while serving.

Serves 10–12.

Kay Larson,
Tyee

Chili Relleno Appetizers

1 (4-oz) can green chilies
3 c grated Monterey Jack
  cheese
1⅓ c grated sharp Cheddar
  cheese

4 eggs
3 tbsp milk
t tbsp flour

Cut the chilies into thin strips. In a lightly greased 9" pan, layer the cheese and chilies, ending with a layer of cheese. Beat the eggs, milk and flour together and pour over the layered ingredients. Bake at 375° for about ½ hour or until firm. Cut into small squares and serve warm.

Gwen Thompson,
Tyee

Tiropitakia

Cheese-filled triangles

5 eggs
½ lb feta cheese
1 pt small-curd cottage
  cheese

1 lb phyllo pastry sheets
1 c butter, melted
½ c olive oil

Beat the eggs until stiff. Add the feta cheese and cottage cheese and mix. Working with 1 pastry sheet at a time and keeping the others covered with a damp cloth, cut the phyllo into 1½" x 15" strips. Combine the melted butter and oil and brush each strip generously. Place 1 tsp cheese mixture at one end of the strip. Fold the corner over to make a triangle, then continue folding until the entire strip is used. Brush each triangle with the butter/oil mixture and place on a greased baking sheet. Bake in a 350° oven for 20 minutes or until golden brown. Serve warm. Tiropitakia may be frozen and baked as needed.

Makes about 50.

Cleo E. Blackstone,
Administrative Staff

Spanakopites

Spinach Cheese Puffs

1 medium onion, finely chopped
¼ c olive oil
1 pkg frozen chopped spinach, thawed, or 1 lb spinach, washed and finely chopped

½ lb feta cheese
6 oz cottage
3 eggs, beaten
¼ c bread crumbs
½ lb phyllo pastry sheets
½ c butter, melted

Sauté the onion in the olive oil for 5 minutes. Add the spinach, which has been thoroughly drained. Simmer with the onion over low heat, stirring occasionally, until most of the moisture is evaporated. In a separate bowl, crumble the feta cheese into small pieces. Add the cottage cheese and blend well. Add the beaten eggs and mix thoroughly. Toss the bread crumbs into the spinach/onion mixture and add the the cheese. Stir until well blended. Working with 1 pastry sheet at a time and keeping the others covered with a damp cloth, cut the phyllo into 1½" x 15" strips. Brush each strip generously with melted butter. Place 1 tsp filling at one end of the strip. Fold the corner over to make a triangle, then continue folding until the entire strip is used. Brush each triangle with butter and place on a greased baking sheet. Bake at 425° for 20 minutes or until golden brown, turning once. Allow the triangles to cool for 5 minutes before serving. If spinach rolls are preferred, cut phyllo sheets into strips and place 1 tbsp filling 1" from the edge of the buttered pastry. Roll to the end. Brush each roll with butter and bake. This recipe may also be made with pie dough in a pie pan and served in wedges.

Makes 25.

Cleo E. Blackstone,
Administrative Staff

Dolmathes

Stuffed Grape Leaves

50 grape leaves, canned
  or fresh
2 lb ground chuck
1 large onion, grated
3 tbsp butter
½ tsp garlic powder
1 tsp salt
½ tbsp pepper

½ tsp pepper
1 tbsp parsley flakes
2 tsp dill weed
½ c rice
1 c olive oil
Juice of 4 or 5 lemons
1 c boiling water

Rinse the grape leaves and drain. Place the meat in a bowl. Brown the onion in the butter in a saucepan. Then, add the garlic powder, salt, pepper, parsley flakes and dill weed and mix thoroughly. Add this mixture and the rice to the meat and mix thoroughly. Place 1 tsp of the mixture in the middle of a grape leaf with the shiny side on the outside and fold securely. Complete filling and folding each leaf. Place the filled leaves in a dutch oven with the folded side down. Pour olive oil and lemon juice over the dolmathes. Add the boiling water to the pan. Place a plate directly over the dolmathes. (The plate remains throughout the cooking time.) Cover the pan with a lid and bring to a boil. Lower to medium heat and cook for 30 minutes. Dolmathes may be served as an appetizer or a side dish.

Makes 50.

Cleo E. Blackstone,
Administrative Staff

Hot Artichoke Spread

Delicious!

1 large can artichoke hearts,
  drained and chopped
1 c mayonnaise

1 c Parmesan cheese
½ tsp garlic powder

Combine all the ingredients and spoon into a small greased casserole. Bake at 350° for 20 minutes and serve hot with crackers.

Helen (Mrs. Martin) Brace,
Tyee

Bacon-Wrapped Water Chestnuts

1 (8-oz) can whole water
   chestnuts
1 lb bacon slices

1 c ketchup
1½ c sugar

Wrap each water chestnut in ½ slice of bacon, secure with a tooth-pick and place on a broiler pan. Broil for 15 minutes on a low rack. Mix the ketchup and sugar and stir over low heat until dissolved. Place the chestnuts in the sauce. Let stand at least 1 hour before serving.

Makes 15.

Dorie Stanton,
Tyee

Zucchini Pickles

Very crisp. Similar to watermelon pickles.

6 large zucchini, peeled,
   seeded and cut in 1" cubes
1 c hydrated lime
1 gallon water

6 c vinegar
10 c sugar
2½ tbsp pickling spice

Dissolve the lime in the water. Soak the zucchini in the lime water for 24 hours in a glass, enamel or plastic container, stirring often. Drain the lime water, then rinse the zucchini in cold water for 10–15 minutes. Dry on towels for 3 hours. In a large stainless steel or enamel kettle, combine the vinegar and sugar, stirring well until the sugar is dissolved. Add the spice and zucchini and allow to stand for 24 hours, stirring often. Bring to a rolling boil for 35 minutes. Add food coloring if desired. Pack in sterile jars and seal. (Formula: 1⅔ c sugar to 1 c vinegar.)

Makes 8 pt.

Edna Steen,
Tyee

Bon Appétit Dip aux Herbes

This dip may also be used as a filling for marinated mushrooms or bite-size tart shells.

1 (8-oz) pkg cream cheese
(room temperature)
6 tbsp milk or cream
1 tsp chicken bouillon
1 tbsp hot water
1 tbsp instant minced onion

½ tsp Bon Appétit
½ tsp marjoram leaves
½ tsp tarragon leaves
½ c finely minced, cooked
chicken, shrimp, clams or
crab meat

Beat the cream cheese until smooth. Gradually stir in the milk or cream and the bouillon which has been dissolved in the hot water. Add all the remaining ingredients, mixing well. Serve with an assortment of crisp crackers or chips.

Valerie Pease,
Tyee

Papaya Appetizer

2 papayas
1 c shrimp or crab
1 lime, sliced
4 slices Pumpernickel bread

Sauce:
½ c mayonnaise
½ c sour cream
Dash of curry
Lime juice

For the Sauce: Combine the mayonnaise, sour cream and curry. Add enough lime juice to make a paste.

Cut each papaya in half. Remove the seeds and the root end. Scoop out the pulp with a melon baller and reserve the skins. Mix the papaya with the seafood, then return the mixture to the skins, or serve it in sherbet glasses. Top the servings with the sauce and serve with a slice of lime and hot pumpernickel bread.

Serves 4.

Dorothy (Mrs. Marv) Harshman,
Coaching Staff

Cocktail Chicken Wings

3 lb chicken wings
3 eggs
¼ c cornstarch
1 tsp garlic salt
1 tsp Accent

Sauce:
¾ c sugar
1 tsp salt
¼ c pineapple juice
¼ c vinegar
1 tbsp soy sauce
4 tbsp ketchup

Cut and discard the tips of the chicken wings. Cut each in half, then sprinkle with the garlic salt and Accent. Let the wings stand for several hours. Beat the eggs. Dip the wings in the egg, then in the cornstarch. Brown the wings in a skillet and place in a casserole. Mix all sauce ingredients in a saucepan and warm thoroughly. Pour the sauce over the chicken wings. Bake at 350° for 1 hour.

Pat Oswald,
Administrative Staff

Sweet and Sour Salmon

*Excellent as an appetizer, side dish for a buffet or
served with potato salad.*

4 lb salmon, boned and cut
  in chunks
1 large jar mixed sweet
  pickles

1 (16-oz) bottle ketchup
1 large onion, sliced

Place the salmon in a dutch oven and add the remaining ingredients. Simmer for 45 minutes. Remove the skin from the salmon while it is still warm. The salmon keeps for 2–3 weeks in the refrigerator.

Serves 12.

Dorothy Crawford,
Tyee

Hot Crab Meat Puffs

2 egg whites
1 c mayonnaise
1 c flaked crab meat

Melba toast rounds
Paprika

Whip the egg whites until stiff. Fold in the mayonnaise and flaked crab meat. Spoon the mixture onto the melba toast rounds and sprinkle each with paprika. Broil until fluffy and lightly browned, about 3 minutes.

Serves 6–8.

Viv Crane,
Tyee

Hot Crab Dip

This is a delicious dip with raw vegetables.

1 can crab meat
2 (8-oz) pkg cream cheese
2 tsp horseradish

1 c mayonnaise
½ c small onion, chopped
½ c grated Parmesan cheese

Mix all the ingredients except Parmesan cheese until smooth. Place in a pie pan and sprinkle with the Parmesan cheese. Bake at 350° for 20–30 minutes, until golden, or cook in a microwave for 6 minutes.

Judy McGrew,
Tyee

Shrimp Puffs

1 lb fresh shrimp
8-10 water chestnuts,
   finely chopped
1 tsp cornstarch

1 tsp sweet white wine
½ tsp salt
1 egg, slightly beaten

Clean and finely chop the shrimp. Mix with all the other ingredients and shape into dollar-size round balls. Fry the balls in deep oil until golden brown, then drain on absorbent paper.

Makes 16.

Ron "Cookie" Jackson,
Athlete

Crab/Cheese Canapé

This is really our favorite. It is so simple that it is ideal for the working woman or man and requires minimum preparation.

1 (8 oz) pkg cream cheese
½–¾ c seafood sauce

½ lb crab or shrimp
Parsley, chopped

Spread the cream cheese over the bottom of a 9" Pyrex pie plate. Over this spread the seafood sauce. Top with the crab or shrimp, or a combination of both. Set the plate on a tray and surround with an assortment of crackers. Garnish the dip with chopped parsley.

Alma Griffin,
Tyee

Shrimp Dip

¼ c milk
¼ c mayonnaise
2 tbsp lemon juice
1 (8 oz) pkg cream cheese,
  softened

2 tbsp finely chopped
  green onion
½ tsp Tabasco sauce
1 c cooked fresh shrimp

Beat the milk, mayonnaise, lemon juice and softened cream cheese until smooth. Mix in the onion, Tabasco and shrimp. Chill for at least 1½ hours. Serve with assorted crackers and fresh vegetables.

Makes 1½ c.

Janice Dewar,
Tyee

Salmon Party Ball

1 (1-lb) can salmon
1 (8-oz) pkg cream cheese
  softened
1 tbsp lemon juice
2 tsp grated onion

1 tsp prepared horseradish
¼ tsp salt
¼ tsp liquid smoke
½ c chopped pecans
3 tbsp minced parsley

Drain and flake the salmon, removing any skin and bones. Combine the salmon, cream cheese, lemon juice, onion, horseradish, salt and liquid smoke, mixing thoroughly. Chill for several hours. Combine the pecans and parsley. Shape the salmon mixture into a ball; roll it in the nut mixture and chill well. Serve with assorted crackers.

Sue Winters,
Athlete

Hot Crab Meat Appetizer

2-3 shallots
2 bay leaves
Pinch of thyme
Pinch of cayenne
1 tsp salt
⅓ c butter
1 lb crab meat

½ c white wine
1 egg
1 tbsp chopped parsley
½ c bread crumbs
1 (14-oz) can artichoke
  bottoms
Hollandaise sauce

Sauté the shallots, bay leaves, thyme, cayenne and salt in the butter. Add the crab meat, wine, egg, parsley and bread crumbs. Place a tbsp of stuffing on each artichoke bottom. Bake in a 350° oven for 15 minutes. Top with hollandaise sauce and serve.

Makes 8.

Lucille M. (Mrs. Earl C.) Jones,
Tyee

Hot Crab Hors d'Oeuvres

1 (8-oz) pkg cream cheese
1 tbsp plus 1 tsp sherry
2 tbsp finely chopped onion
½ tbsp horseradish
¼ tsp salt

¼ tsp pepper
½ lb fresh crab or
   1 (7½-oz) can crab meat
Slivered almonds

Thoroughly cream together the cream cheese, sherry, onion, horseradish, salt and pepper. Add the crab and mix well. Place this mixture in a buttered casserole. Sprinkle with slivered almonds and bake in a 375° oven for 15 minutes. Serve hot. Dip with Triskets, Wheat Thins or potato chips.

Makes 2 c.

Frances Vaughn,
Tyee

Hot Crab Dip

1 (8-oz) pkg cream cheese
1½ c or 1 (6½-oz) can crab
   meat
2 tbsp finely chopped onion
1 tbsp milk

½ tsp cream-style
   horseradish
¼ tsp salt
Dash of pepper
⅓ c slivered almonds

Soften the cream cheese and add the remaining ingredients. Spoon the mixture into an ovenproof dish. Top with the almonds and bake at 375° for 15 minutes, or put the mixture into a chafing dish, heat and serve.

Makes 2 c.

Joan (Mrs. Robert G.) Waldo,
Vice Provost's wife

Mint Julep

Sip slowly and savor.

12 fresh mint leaves
1 ½ tsp sugar
Water

Ice, finely crushed
Bourbon whiskey

Place 12 or more mint leaves in the bottom of a tall glass. Cover with the sugar and a small amount of water. Crush the mixture into a sweet syrup. The syrup should be quite strong. If it is not flavored properly, add more leaves and sugar. Fill the glass with crushed ice, then bourbon. Stir until the glass frosts. Be careful, while mixing, to keep your fingers at the top of the glass or the frosting will not be uniform. Garnish with 2–3 mint sprigs and serve.

T. Evans Wyckoff,
Tyee

Pineapple/Cheese Ball

2 (8-oz) pkg cream cheese,
  softened
1 (8¼-oz) can crushed
  pineapple, drained
1 c chopped macadamia nuts

¼ c finely chopped green
  pepper
2 tbsp finely chopped onions
1 tbsp seasoned salt

In a small electric mixer bowl, beat the cream cheese until smooth. Gradually stir in the pineapple, ½ the nuts and all the green pepper, onion and salt. Shape the mixture into a ball. Cover with remaining nuts. Refrigerate overnight. Serve with butter crackers.

Mereda Metz,
Tyee

BREADS

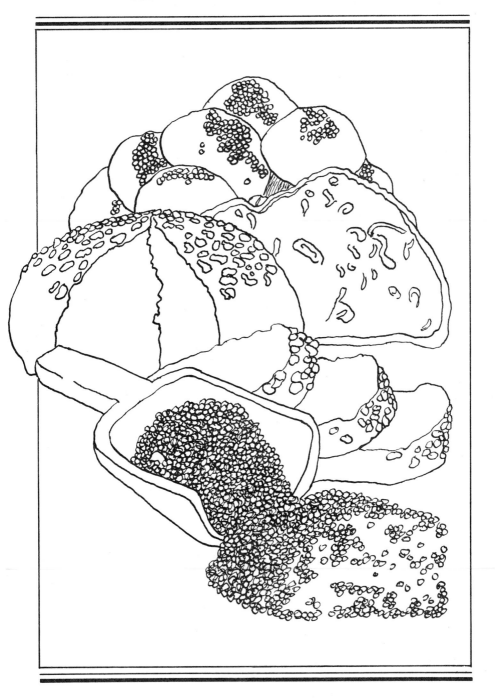

White Bread

½ c powdered milk
3 c hot water
¼ c vegetable oil
¼ c sugar
4 tsp salt

2 pkg dry yeast
1 c warm water (115°)
2 tsp sugar
9–10 c flour

Mix the milk, hot water, oil, sugar and salt together. Set aside. Combine the yeast, warm water and sugar together and let stand for 10 minutes. Combine the two mixtures and add flour, 1 c at a time, mixing thoroughly. On a well-floured board, knead the dough for 10 minutes until satiny. Place in a greased bowl, cover with a damp cloth and let rise until doubled in size. Punch the dough down and form into loaves and place in greased 9" x 5" pans. Bake at 350° for 25 minutes, until brown and crusty on top.

Makes 3–4 loaves.

Marilyn (Mrs. David F.) Ludwig, Tyee

Whole Wheat and Oat Bread

2 pkg dry yeast
3 c warm water
⅓ c molasses
¼ c vegetable oil

1½ tbsp salt
⅔ rolled oats
7½–8 c whole wheat flour

Sprinkle the yeast into the water in a large bowl. Stir until the yeast dissolves. Add the molasses and stir. Leave the mixture undisturbed until bubbly, about 10 minutes. Stir the oil, salt, rolled oats and 4 c flour into the yeast mixture, beating until smooth. Slowly beat in remaining 3 c flour to make a stiff dough. Turn the dough onto a lightly floured surface. Knead it until smooth and elastic, about 10 minutes, using only as much flour as needed to keep the dough from sticking. Place the dough in a greased bowl, turning it to grease all sides. Cover with a towel and let rise in a warm place, for 1 hour or until doubled in bulk. Punch the dough down, then turn it out onto a lightly floured surface. Knead it a few times, then divide it in half. Invert the bowl over the dough, and let it rest for about 10 minutes. Shape the dough into 2 loaves. Place the loaves in 2 lightly greased

9" x 5" pans. Let it rise in a warm place for 45 minutes or until doubled in bulk. Bake at 350° for 1 hour and 10 minutes, or until browned and loaves sound hollow when tapped. Remove from the pans to wire racks to cool completely.

Makes 2 loaves.

Leslie Coaston,
Athlete

Black Russian Rye Bread

4 c unsifted rye flour
3 c unsifted white flour
1 tsp sugar
2 tsp salt
2 c whole bran cereal
2 tbsp caraway seed, crushed
½ tsp fennel seed, crushed
2 tsp onion powder
2 tsp instant coffee

2 pkg dry yeast
2½ c water
¼ c vinegar
¼ c dark molasses
1 sq unsweetened chocolate
¼ c butter
1 tsp cornstarch in ½ c cold
    water

Combine the rye and white flours. In a large bowl, mix 2½ c flour mixture, sugar, salt, cereal, caraway, fennel seed, onion, coffee and undissolved yeast. In a separate saucepan, combine 2½ c water, vinegar, molasses, chocolate and butter and heat over low heat to 120°–130°. The butter and chocolate do not need to melt. Gradually add to the dry ingredients, mixing well. Stir in enough of the remaining flour mixture to make a soft dough. Cover and let stand for 10 minutes. Turn onto a floured board and knead until smooth and elastic. Place in a greased bowl, cover and let rise until double, about 1½ hours. Punch down. Return the dough to the floured board. Divide in half and shape into balls about 5" in diameter. Place each in a greased 8" round cake pan. Cover, then let rise until doubled. Bake at 350° for 45 minutes, until done. Cook the cornstarch and water until the mixture boils, stirring constantly. Brush the bread with cornstarch mixture when baked, then return the bread to the oven for 3 minutes until the glaze is set.

Makes 2 loaves.

Marilyn (Mrs. David F.) Ludwig,
Tyee

Beer Bread

3 c self-rising flour
3 tbsp sugar

1 (12-oz) can Budweiser
beer

Mix all the ingredients quickly and thoroughly. Place in a greased loaf pan. Bake at 350° for 1 hour.

Jan Hurworth,
Tyee

Irish Soda Bread

"Pile the butter on the hot slices. Yum!!"

4 c flour
1 tsp salt
1 tbsp baking powder
1 tsp baking soda
¼ c plus 2 tbsp sugar

¼ c butter
2 c raisins or currants
1 egg
1¾ c buttermilk

Combine the flour, salt, baking powder, baking soda and sugar. Cut the butter in until crumbly, then add the raisins. Beat the egg with the buttermilk and add to the butter/flour mixture. Turn the dough onto a floured board and knead 2–3 minutes. Divide into 2 round loaves and place them on cookie sheets or pie plates. Cut a cross about ½" deep through the middle of the loaves. Bake at 375° for 35–40 minutes.

Gloria Oswald Ehrig,
Tyee

Contagious Cornbread

1 onion, peeled and sliced
¼ c butter
1½ c cornbread mix
1 egg, beaten
⅓ c milk
1 can creamed corn

2 dashes of Tabasco sauce
1 c sour cream
¼ tsp salt
¼ tsp dill weed
1 c grated sharp Cheddar
cheese

Sauté the onion in the butter, then set aside. Combine the cornbread mix, egg, milk, corn and Tabasco. Pour into an 8" x 8" buttered pan. Mix the sour cream, salt, dill weed and ½ the cheese with the onions and pour over the cornbread mixture. Sprinkle with remaining cheese. Bake at 425° for 25–30 minutes. Let set 20 minutes before serving. Cut in squares.

Vicki (Mrs. Frank W.) Crealock,
Tyee

Jalapeño Cornbread

2½ c cornmeal
1 c flour
2 tbsp sugar
1 tbsp salt
4 tsp baking powder
3 eggs
1½ c milk

½ c cooking oil
1 (1-lb) can creamed corn
6–8 jalapeño chili peppers,
    chopped
2 c grated sharp cheese
1 large onion, grated

In a bowl, stir together the cornmeal, flour, sugar, salt and baking powder. In a separate bowl, beat the eggs lightly, then stir in the milk and cooking oil. Add the liquid mixture to the cornmeal mixture and stir in the creamed corn, peppers, cheese and onion. Pour the batter into 2 greased 9" x 11" baking pans and bake in a 425° oven for 25 minutes or until it tests done.

Fletcher Jenkins,
Athlete

Sunflower Seed Bread

3 c sifted all-purpose flour
1 c sugar
1 tsp salt
3½ tsp baking powder
1 egg, beaten
¾ c orange juice

4 tsp grated orange peel
¾ c milk
¼ c butter or margarine,
  melted
¾ c roasted sunflower seeds

Sift the flour, sugar, salt and baking powder together. Combine the egg, orange juice, peel, milk and butter. Add to the dry ingredients, mixing well. Stir in the sunflower seeds. Pour into a 9" x 5" x 2" pan. Bake at 350° for 1 hour. Cool for 15 minutes before removing from the pan.

Makes 1 loaf.

Marilyn S. Peterson,
Tyee

Crusty Whole Wheat Rolls

2 pkg yeast
1½ c lukewarm water
1 tsp salt
1 tbsp sugar

2 c whole wheat flour
White flour
Cornmeal

Dissolve the yeast in the lukewarm water and stir in the salt and sugar. With a wooden spoon, stir in the whole wheat flour, 1 c at a time, beating thoroughly after each addition. Add enough white flour to make a soft but firm dough. Shape the dough into a ball and cover it with a cloth. Let it rise in a warm place until it is doubled in size. Punch the dough down and shape it into small round rolls. Put the rolls on a baking sheet liberally sprinkled with cornmeal and let them rise for 5 minutes. Brush the rolls with cold water and put them in a cold oven. Set the oven to 400° and put a large flat pan filled with boiling water on a rack below the baking sheet. Bake the rolls for about 40 minutes or until they are lightly browned and crusty.

Makes 4 dozen.

Scott Garnett,
Athlete

Angel Biscuits

1 pkg dry yeast
2 tbsp warm water
5 c flour
1 tbsp baking powder
1 tsp baking soda

2 tsp salt
2 tbsp sugar
1 c shortening
2 c buttermilk

Dissolve the yeast in warm water. Sift the dry ingredients into a large bowl, then cut in the shortening. Add the buttermilk and yeast. Knead for 1 minute. Roll to ½" thickness and cut with a biscuit cutter. Bake the biscuits on a greased pan at 425° for 12–15 minutes.

Makes 2 dozen.

Marie (Mrs. Robert) Ridgeway, Tyee

Guastelle

Italian Rolls

2⅓ c water
½ c oil
¼ c sugar
1 tbsp salt

2 pkg yeast
2 large eggs
6 c flour

Heat 2 c water to boiling. Pour the water over the oil, sugar and salt and let cool until the mixture is lukewarm. Dissolve the yeast in ⅓ c warm water. Add the yeast to the cooled mixture, along with the eggs and ½ the flour. Stir until smooth. Blend in the remaining flour. Knead the dough lightly on a floured board. Shape into rolls and place on buttered cookie sheets. Let rise until doubled. The rolls may be brushed with egg white and sprinkled with poppy or sesame seeds. Bake at 375°–400° for 15–20 minutes, or until golden brown.

Makes 2 dozen.

Sharon (Mrs. Floyd) Jackson, Tyee

No-Knead Refrigerator Rolls

2 pkg dry yeast
2 c warm water
½ c sugar
2 eggs, beaten

⅞ c oil
2 tsp salt
6½–7 c flour

Dissolve the yeast in the warm water. Add the sugar, eggs, oil and salt; stir well. Add the flour gradually. Place the dough in a greased bowl, turning once to grease the surface. Cover tightly and refrigerate until needed. The dough will keep in the refrigerator for 5–6 days. Shape into rolls and place in greased muffin pans. Let rise until double in size, about 1½–2 hours. Bake at 400° for 12–15 minutes.

Makes 2 dozen.

Marie (Mrs. Robert) Ridgeway,
Tyee

Refrigerator Herb Rolls

Good with poultry.

1 pkg active dry yeast
3¼–3½ c sifted flour
2 tsp celery seed
1 tsp dried thyme

1¼ c milk
¼ c butter or margarine
1 tsp salt
1 egg

In a large mixing bowl, combine the yeast, 1½ c flour, celery seed and thyme. In a saucepan, heat the milk, butter and salt until just warm, stirring constantly. Add to the dry mixture. Add the egg and beat at low speed for ½ minute, then 3 minutes at high speed. Stir in enough of the remaining flour to make a soft dough. Use a wooden spoon at the end if necessary. Place in a greased bowl, turning once to grease the top of the dough. Cover and chill for at least 3 hours or up to 2 days. Shape into 18 cloverleaf rolls by placing 3 walnut-size balls in each of 18 greased muffin tins. Brush with butter and let rise, covered, until doubled in size. Bake at 400° for 12–15 minutes.

Makes 18 rolls.

Gail (Mrs. Bruce) Richards,
Tyee

Quick (Food Processor) Butter Croissants

5 c all-purpose flour
1 c butter, refrigerated
1 pkg dry yeast
1 c warm water
¾ c evaporated milk

1½ tsp salt
⅓ c sugar
2 eggs
¼ c butter, melted

Fit the metal blade into a food processor, and put in 4 c flour. Cut the butter into ½" squares and distribute over the flour. Process, using on-off bursts, until the butter particles are the size of peas. Transfer the mixture to a large mixing bowl. Process the yeast and water with 2 on-off bursts. Add the milk, salt, sugar, 1 egg and the remaining 1 c flour. Add the melted butter and process until the batter is smooth. Pour the batter over the butter/flour mixture. With a spatula, carefully fold the mixture until all the flour is moistened. Cover with plastic wrap and refrigerate for at least 4 hours or up to 4 days. Turn the dough onto a floured board, press it into a ball and knead briefly to release any air. Divide the dough into 4 equal parts. Shape 1 part at a time, leaving the remaining dough in the refrigerator. Roll 1 portion of the dough into a 14" circle. With a sharp knife, cut into 8 equal wedges. Loosely roll each wedge from the wide end toward the point. Curve into a crescent and place, point side down, on an ungreased baking sheet. Repeat until all croissants are shaped, placing them 1½" apart. Cover lightly and let rise at room temperature in a draft-free place. When almost doubled in size (about 2 hours), brush with the remaining egg beaten with 1 tbsp water. Bake in a 325° oven for 35 minutes or until lightly browned. Serve warm or let cool on racks.

Makes 32 croissants.

Kay Richards,
Tyee

French Breakfast Puffs

⅓ c soft shortening, part
  butter
1 c sugar
1 egg
1½ c sifted flour
1½ tsp baking powder

½ tsp salt
¼ tsp nutmeg
½ c milk
⅓ c butter, melted
1 tsp cinnamon

Mix shortening, ½ c sugar and egg thoroughly. Sift together the flour, baking powder, salt and nutmeg. Stir into the sugar mixture alternately with the milk. Fill greased muffin cups ⅔ full. Bake in a 350° preheated oven for 20–25 minutes, or until golden brown. Immediately roll the muffins in the melted butter, then in a mixture of the remaining ½ c sugar and the cinnamon. Serve hot.

Makes 12 muffins.

Bette (Mrs. Ronald W.) Sholund,
Tyee

Nut Muffins

½ c butter
1 c brown sugar
1 egg
1 c milk

½ tsp baking soda
½ c chopped walnuts
1 tsp vanilla
2 scant c flour

Combine all the ingredients, mixing thoroughly. Fill 12 greased muffin tins almost to the top with the batter. Cover with waxed paper and let stand overnight. Bake at 400° for 30 minutes.

Makes 1 dozen.

Gail (Mrs. Bruce) Richards,
Tyee

Whole Grain Muffins

2 c whole wheat flour
1 c whole bran cereal
¼ c instant nonfat dry milk
3 tbsp baking powder

¼ tsp salt
1 c milk
⅓ c honey
¼ c vegetable oil

Combine the flour, bran, dry milk, baking powder and salt in a large bowl. Make a well in the center of the mixture. Combine the milk, honey and oil, then pour the mixture into the well. Mix just until the dry ingredients are moistened. Fill greased 2½" muffin cups ⅔ full. Bake at 400° for 12 minutes.

Makes 1½ dozen.

Ken Shannon,
Coaching Staff

Helen Swope's Graham Bread

Helen Swope owned and operated a very successful and popular tea room in the White-Henry-Stuart Building during the '30s and served this bread always. She gave my mother the recipe.

2 c graham flour
1 c whole wheat flour
½ c sugar

1 tsp salt
2 tsp baking soda
2 c buttermilk

Sift together the dry ingredients. Add the buttermilk and mix thoroughly. Pour the batter into a greased loaf pan. Bake for 1 hour in an oven preheated to 400° but reduced to 350° while bread is baking.

Makes 1 loaf.

Sylvia Patterson,
Administrative Staff

Best-Ever Banana Bread

5 large bananas	3½ c flour
4 eggs, well beaten	2 tsp baking soda
1 c shortening	1 tsp salt
2 c sugar	1 c chopped walnuts

Mash the bananas thoroughly and add the eggs. In a separate bowl, cream the shortening, then gradually add the sugar and beat until fluffy. Add the banana mixture. Combine the flour, soda and salt and blend into the batter. Stir in the walnuts. Bake in 2 greased loaf pans at 300° for 1¼ hours or until firm to the touch.

Makes 2 loaves.

Ruby (Mrs. Gordon E.) Smith, Tyee

Banana Bread

½ c shortening	2 c flour
1¼ c sugar	1 tsp baking powder
2 eggs	1 tsp baking soda
1 c mashed banana (approx 3 fruits)	¼ tsp salt
½ tsp vanilla	½ c chopped nuts
½ c sour cream	½ tsp cinnamon

Cream the shortening and 1 c sugar until light and fluffy. Beat in the eggs, bananas and vanilla. Fold in the sour cream. Sift together the flour, baking powder, soda and salt. Fold into the sugar mixture, then stir to blend. Mix together the nuts, remaining ¼ c sugar and cinnamon. Sprinkle ½ this mixture into the bottom of a well-greased loaf pan. Spoon in ½ the batter. Sprinkle the remaining cinnamon mixture and top with the remaining batter. Bake at 350° for 45 minutes or until a toothpick inserted in the center comes out clean.

Makes 1 loaf.

Chuck Nelson, Athlete

Banana Muffins

1¼ bananas
1 c plus 2 tbsp sugar
¼ c oil
2 eggs

2¼ c cake flour
½ c all-purpose flour
1 tbsp baking soda
½ c buttermilk

In a bowl, mash the bananas with a fork and mix in the sugar. Mix in the oil and eggs, then the 2 flours and the baking soda. Stir in the buttermilk until all the dry particles are moistened and the batter is mixed but still slightly lumpy. Fill about 18 medium muffin tins ⅔ full. The pans may be lightly buttered, or paper liners may be used. Bake at 400° for 16–18 minutes, or until a toothpick inserted in the center of a muffin comes out clean.

Makes 18.

Bruce Kroon,
Athlete

Mom's Blueberry Muffins

2 c sifted all-purpose flour
1 tbsp baking powder
½ tsp salt
⅓ c sugar

1 c fresh or frozen blueberries
1 egg
1 c milk
4 tbsp butter, melted

Sift the flour, baking powder, salt and sugar together. Fold in the blueberries. Beat the egg and milk together and lightly mix with the blueberry mixture. Fold the melted butter into the batter. Bake in greased muffin tins at 425° for about 25 minutes. Serve warm with butter.

Makes 12–15 muffins.

Steve Pelluer,
Athlete

Mango Bread

2 c flour
1 c sugar
2 tsp baking soda
1 tsp salt
2 tsp cinnamon
3 eggs

½ c oil
⅓ c butter, melted
2 large mangoes, cubed
1 tsp vanilla
½ c raisins (optional)
½ c chopped nuts (optional)

Sift together the flour, sugar, baking soda, salt and cinnamon; set aside. Beat the eggs, oil, butter, mangoes and vanilla together. Add the flour mixture and beat well. Mix in the raisins and nuts if desired. Bake at 350° for 1 hour or until a toothpick inserted in the loaf comes out clean.

Makes 2 small loaves
or 1 large loaf.

Mary Lou (Mrs Walter) Hinds,
Tyee

Mango Bread

2½ c diced mangoes
1 tbsp lemon juice
2 c flour
1½ tsp cinnamon
1½ tsp baking soda
½ tsp salt

1¼ c sugar
½ c nuts, chopped
½ c raisins, chopped
½ c shredded coconut
3 eggs
¾ c salad oil

Marinate the diced mangoes in lemon juice. Sift the flour, cinnamon, soda, salt and sugar together. Add the nuts, raisins and coconut and set aside. Beat the eggs and add the oil, then the mangoes. Stir the mango mixture quickly and lightly into the dry ingredients. Pour the batter into 2 greased 8½" x 4½" loaf pans dusted with flour. Bake in a preheated 325° oven for 45–60 minutes. Test with a toothpick.

Makes 2 loaves.

Helen Paschall,
Tyee

BRUNCH

Dutch Babies

1 ½ c milk
1 ½ c flour
6 eggs

1 ½ tbsp sugar
Dash of salt
8–9 tbsp butter

Combine the milk and flour. Beat in the eggs, 1 at a time. Add the sugar and salt. Put 1 tbsp butter in each of several small Pyrex dishes. Place in a 400° oven until the butter melts. Pour equal amounts of batter into each dish, approximately ¾" deep. Bake for 15 minutes at 400°. Lower heat to 300° and bake for another 15 minutes. Remove from the baking dishes. Serve with powdered sugar and lemon juice or maple syrup.

Makes 8–9.

Jim Calderhead,
Tyee

Surprise Breakfast Casserole

1 lb Italian seasoned sausage
8 to 10 slices bread,
  crusts removed
½ c chopped celery
½ c chopped green pepper
½ c diced green chilies

2 tbsp grated onion
4 eggs, slightly beaten
3 c milk
1 can cream of
  mushroom soup
1 c grated Monterey Jack cheese

Line the bottom of a 9" x 13" casserole with half the bread. Brown the sausage in a skillet and drain any excess fat. Scatter the sausage and then the vegetables over the bread. Cover with the remaining bread. Mix together the eggs and milk and pour into the casserole. Refrigerate the casserole overnight. Bake at 325° for 45 minutes. Remove the casserole from the oven and cover it with the soup. Sprinkle the cheese over the soup and return it to the oven for 15 minutes more.

Serves 8-10.

Feathers Cereghino,
Tyee

Sausage and Egg Casserole

8 slices white bread
2 lb link sausages
4 eggs
2½ c milk

1 can cream of
mushroom soup
¾ lb sharp Cheddar
cheese, grated

Trim and cube the bread. Line the bottom of a buttered casserole with the bread cubes. Brown the sausages and cut into thirds. Place the sausage pieces over the bread in the casserole. Beat the eggs, then add the milk and soup. Pour the egg mixture over the sausage. Sprinkle with the Cheddar cheese. Cover the casserole with foil and refrigerate overnight. Remove the casserole from the refrigerator 30 minutes before baking. Bake, covered, at 325° for 1½ hours.

Serves 6.

Marlene Johnson,
Tyee

Sausage-Sunflower Seed Squares

12 eggs
1½ c sour cream
1 tsp salt
½ c minced fresh parsley
4 green onions with tops
   finely chopped

1 (4-oz) can Vienna
   sausages, thinly sliced
1½ c grated Swiss cheese
¼ c margarine, melted
½ c toasted sunflower seeds,
   divided

Beat the eggs with a whisk until blended. Stir in all the other ingredients except ¼ cup sunflower seeds. Pour into a greased 10½" x 15½" jellyroll pan. Sprinkle with the remaining seeds. Bake in a 350° preheated oven for about 25 minutes. Cut into squares to serve. This dish may be made 1 day ahead and heated in a 350° oven for about 15 minutes, until warmed through.

Serves 10-12.

Jeanne Calderhead,
Tyee

Sausage-Filled Crêpes

Filling:
1 lb bulk sausage
¼ c chopped onion
½ c grated Cheddar cheese
1 (3-oz) pkg cream cheese
¼ tsp marjoram

Crêpes:
3 eggs, beaten
1 c plus 1 tbsp milk
1 tbsp oil
1 c flour
½ tsp salt

Sauce:
½ c sour cream
¼ c butter or margarine, softened

For the filling: Cook the sausage and onion. Drain and add the Cheddar cheese, cream cheese and marjoram, mixing well. Set aside.

For the Crêpes: Combine the eggs, milk and oil. Add the flour and salt; beat until smooth. Pour 2 tbsp batter in a greased 6" skillet. Tilt so that the batter spreads evenly. Cook on 1 side for 1 minute and invert onto paper towling. Makes 16 crêpes.

For the sauce: Thoroughly mix the sour cream and butter. Place 2 tbsp filling down the center of each crêpe and roll it up. Place in a baking dish, then cover and chill. Bake, covered, at 375° for 40 minutes. During the last 5 minutes, spoon the sauce over the crêpes and bake uncovered.

These are also excellent hors d'oeuvres. Cut each crêpe into 4 sections, then roll each piece around a small amount of filling. These crêpes may easily be made ahead and frozen, omitting sauce until ready to serve.

Mary Ann Farmer,
Coaching Staff

MHB's Sunday Buttermilk Pancakes

2 c flour
1 tbsp sugar
1 tbsp corn meal
1 tsp baking powder
1 tsp baking soda

1 tsp salt
2 eggs
2 c buttermilk
2 tbsp butter, melted

In a bowl, sift together the flour, sugar, corn meal, baking powder, baking soda, and salt. In another bowl, beat the eggs lightly and combine them with the buttermilk and melted butter. Pour the buttermilk mixture over the dry ingredients and stir until all the flour is moistened thoroughly. Drop the batter 2 tbsp at a time onto a hot greased griddle and cook the pancakes until bubbles form and break on the top. Turn the pancakes and cook the other side. Serve hot with butter and maple syrup.

Makes about 20 pancakes.

Milton H. Bohart,
Tyee

Pecan Coffee Cake

2 c flour
1 c sugar
½ tsp salt
2 tsp baking powder
1½ tsp cinnamon
½ tsp nutmeg
½ tsp cloves

½ c butter
2 eggs, well beaten
2 tbsp dark molasses
¾ c milk
½ c pecans, halved or
    chopped

Sift the flour, sugar, salt, baking powder, cinnamon, nutmeg and cloves together. With a pastry blender, cut the butter into the sifted ingredients. Set aside ½ c butter/flour mixture. To the rest of the mixture, add the eggs, molasses and milk and beat by hand with a wooden spoon until thoroughly combined. Pour in a 2-qt buttered Pyrex baking dish. Sprinkle the reserved mixture over the top, then the pecans. Bake at 375° for 30 minutes and serve immediately.

Makes 1 cake.

Mildred Ose,
Tyee

Breakfast-Brunch Quiche

2 (9") unbaked pie shells
12 oz bulk sausage, browned
  and drained
8 oz mozzarella
  cheese, grated

8 eggs, beaten
1½ c milk
½ tsp salt
½ tsp pepper

Line the pie shells with the cooked sausage and then the cheese. Combine the eggs, milk, salt, and pepper. Pour ½ the egg mixture into each pie shell. Bake at 375° for 30 minutes.

Serves 8.

Jean B. (Mrs. Tracy) King,
Alumni Director

Impossible Quiche

3 eggs
½ c Bisquick
½ c melted butter
1½ c milk
¼ tsp salt

Dash of pepper
1 c grated Swiss or Monterey
  Jack cheese
½ c cooked, diced ham or
  bacon

Place the eggs, Bisquick, butter, milk, salt and pepper in a blender and blend for only a few seconds. Pour into a greased 9" pie pan. Sprinkle the cheese and meat on top, then push them below the surface with the back of a large spoon. Bake at 350° for 45 minutes. Let cool 10 minutes before serving.

Serves 4.

Dorie Stanton,
Tyee

Ham and Egg Casserole

*This is an old family recipe, passed down from Freddie Biondi.
Serve with fresh fruits, croissants and coffee.*

½ lb ham, chopped
½ lb Swiss cheese, shredded
10 eggs

½ tsp Worcestershire sauce
½ tsp dry mustard
1 c half-and-half

Butter the bottom of 9" x 13" glass casserole. Place the ham and cheese in the casserole. Slightly beat the eggs, then add Worcestershire and half-and-half. Pour the mixture over the ham and cheese. Bake at 350° for 35 minutes.

Serves 6-8.

Judy Biondi,
Director of Athletics-Funding

Sausage and Egg Casserole

3 slices bread, cubed
1 lb sausage
6 eggs
2 c milk
1 tsp salt

1 tsp Worcestershire sauce
Dash of Tabasco sauce
Dash of pepper
1 c grated Cheddar cheese

Mix the bread pieces with the sausage. Beat the eggs, then add the milk and seasonings. Add the egg mixture to the sausage mixture, then add the cheese. Mix well, then refrigerate overnight. Bake in a casserole at 350° for 45 minutes. Remove any excess grease.

Serves 6.

Jean B. (Mrs. Tracy) King,
Alumni Director

Deviled Eggs in Cream

6 eggs, hard-cooked
2 tbsp mayonnaise
3 tbsp butter
2 tbsp flour
1 ½ c light cream

1 egg yolk
Salt and pepper to taste
½ c grated cheese
1 c diced ham

Cut the cooked eggs in half lengthwise. Remove the yolks and mix them with the mayonnaise. Stuff the yolks into the whites. Place the eggs in a shallow baking dish. Melt the butter, then stir in the flour until smooth. Add the cream and cook, stirring constantly, until thickened. Beat a little of the sauce into the egg yolk. Add the yolk mixture to the sauce and mix well. Season with salt and pepper. Pour the sauce over the eggs and sprinkle with cheese and ham. Bake in a 350° oven for 20-25 minutes.

Serves 6.

Hazel (Mrs. G.M.) Whitacre, Tyee

Eggs-Je Ne Sais Pas!

1 ½ dozen eggs, hard-cooked
½ lb bacon
¼ c butter or margarine
¼ c flour
1 c light cream
1 c milk
1 lb sharp Cheddar cheese, grated

¼ tsp thyme
1 clove garlic, crushed
¼ tsp marjoram
¼ tsp basil
¼ c chopped parsley
½ c buttered bread crumbs

Cut the eggs in thin slices. Fry the bacon until crisp, drain and crumble it. Melt the butter over low heat, then slowly mix in the flour, stirring constantly until well blended. Slowly add the cream and milk and stir until thickened. Add the cheese, stirring until melted. Season the sauce with the garlic, thyme, basil, marjoram and parsley. Pour ½ of the sauce into a greased 9" x 13" baking dish. Add the eggs and bacon, then the remaining sauce. Sprinkle with the buttered bread crumbs. Bake at 350° for 20 minutes, or until bubbly.

Serves 10-12.

Jean B. (Mrs. Tracy) King, Alumni Director

J. Michael Kenyon's Incredibly Famous Scrambled Eggs for Two

6 eggs
1 c butter
2 small chili peppers
1 (2-oz) shot glass cream
1 tsp salt

1 tsp pepper
3 oz sharp Cheddar cheese, grated
3 oz mild Swiss cheese, grated

Break the eggs into a medium-size mixing bowl. Melt ½ c butter and add to the eggs. Chop the peppers into little bits and throw them into the mixing bowl. Add the remaining ingredients except for ½ c butter, and whomp everything together. Melt the remaining ½ c butter in a frying pan. Gently pour in the egg mixture and muddle them around until they look well done enough to eat.

Serves 2.

J. Michael Kenyon,
Tyee

Eggs Benoit

8 eggs
1 can cream of chicken soup
1 tbsp dehydrated onion flakes
1 tsp dry mustard

1 tbsp Worcestershire sauce
1 c grated sharp cheese
Salt and pepper to taste
8 English muffins

Break the eggs into a greased 9" pie plate. Mix the remaining ingredients in a saucepan. Heat until warm, then pour the mixture over the eggs. Bake at 350° for 30 minutes. To serve, pour the eggs over English muffins.

Serves 6-8.

Jean B. (Mrs. Tracy) King,
Alumni Director

Eggs Hussarde

2 slices ham, grilled
2 (3") toast rounds
¼ c marchand de vin sauce
  (see following recipe)
2 slices tomato, slightly
  broiled
2 eggs, poached

Paprika
Hollandaise Sauce:
3 egg yolks
2 tbsp lemon juice
½ c butter
Dash of salt
Dash of cayenne

Place 1 slice ham on a toast round. Cover with Marchand de Vin Sauce. Top with a tomato slice and then a poached egg. Ladle Hollandaise sauce over the egg and sprinkle with paprika.

For the Hollandaise sauce: Beat the egg yolks and lemon juice together. Melt the butter in a double boiler, then blend in the egg mixture, salt, and cayenne. Lightly beat the mixture until completely blended.

Serves 2.

Jean B. (Mrs. Tracy) King,
Alumni Director

Marchand de Vin Sauce
For Eggs Hussarde

½ c butter
½ c chopped ham
½ c chopped onion
⅓ c chopped mushrooms
⅓ c chopped shallots

1 tbsp minced garlic
2 tbsp flour
Salt and pepper to taste
¾ c beef broth
1½ c red wine

Sauté the ham, onions, mushrooms, shallots, and garlic in the butter until the vegetables are limp. Add the flour and season with salt and pepper. Cook the mixture over medium heat for about 10 minutes, until it is rich brown in color. Add the beef broth and wine and simmer for 45 minutes, stirring frequently. The sauce will keep in the refrigerator.

Jean B. (Mrs. Tracy) King,
Alumni Director

Recruiting Breakfast Buffet Eggs

1½ dozen eggs
Salt and pepper to taste
1 (8-oz) pkg cream cheese

1 can Aunt Penny's
  white sauce

Break the eggs into a large frying pan. Season with salt and pepper. Cook over low heat until the eggs start to thicken. Break the cream cheese into pieces and add to the eggs. Stir in the white sauce. Continue to cook, stirring occasionally, until set. Garnish with parsley or chives.

Serves 8-10.

Carol (Mrs. Don) James,
Coaching Staff

Recruiting Breakfast Hash Browns

1 (24-oz) pkg frozen
  hash browns
2 c half-and-half

½ c butter, melted
Salt and pepper to taste
½ c grated Parmesan cheese

Partially thaw the potatoes and break into pieces in a greased 9" x 12" pan. Pour the half-and-half over the top of the potatoes, then add the melted butter. Season with salt and pepper and sprinkle with the cheese. Bake at 350° for 1 hour.

Serves 14-16.

Carol (Mrs Don) James,
Coaching Staff

Smoked Salmon Tart

1 unbaked 9" pie shell
1 egg white, lightly beaten
½ lb smoked salmon, chopped
1 c grated Swiss cheese
4 eggs
1¼ c half-and-half

1 tbsp finely minced fresh dill
  or 1 tsp dried dillweed
½ tsp salt
¼ tsp freshly ground pepper
Red caviar (optional)

Brush the pastry shell lightly with the egg white and bake at 400° for 5 minutes. Let cool slightly. Distribute the salmon over the bottom of the pie shell, then sprinkle with the cheese. Beat all the remaining ingredients together except the caviar and pour into the pie shells. Bake at 450° for 15 minutes. Reduce the oven to 350° and continue baking until the top is golden, about 15 minutes. Garnish with caviar.

Serves 6-8.

Stewart Hill,
Athlete

SOUPS

Fish Ragout

A simplified Cioppino

½ c chopped onion
2 to 3 zucchini, thinly sliced
1 clove garlic, minced
2 to 3 carrots, cut in julienne
   strips
2 tbsp polyunsaturated oil
1 can tomato soup
1 can tomato rice soup
2 soup cans water
1 small can stewed tomatoes

2 chicken bouillon cubes
1 tsp salt
¼ tsp thyme
¼ tsp basil
2 tsp minced parsley
⅛ tsp pepper
2 lb fish (combine shrimp,
   scallops, halibut, filet of sole
   and/or crab)

Sauté the onion, garlic, zucchini, and carrots in the oil. Add all the other ingredients, except the fish. Cover and simmer for 20 minutes. Cut the fish into 1" pieces, then add to the stew. Cover and simmer for 5–10 minutes.

Serves 6.

April A. Lundell,
Tyee

Husky Den Fish Chowder

2 oz salt pork or bacon, cut in
   1" cubes
1 large onion, thinly sliced
3 medium-size potatoes
1 lb filet fresh white fish
   (such as sole or halibut)

1½ c boiling water
1 (14½-oz) can evaporated
   milk
2 c milk
Salt and pepper to taste

Place the salt pork or bacon in a heavy pot and cook until brown and crisp. Remove the pork or bacon, then add the onion to the drippings in the pot and slowly cook until golden, about 10 minutes. Peel and dice the potatoes. Cut the fish into 1" cubes. Add the potatoes and fish to the onions. Add the boiling water, then cover and simmer until potatoes are tender, about 15 minutes. Add the milks and salt and pepper, then cover and simmer very gently for 12–15 minutes.

Makes 1½ qt.

Paul Skansi,
Athlete

West Coast Seafood Stew

12 raw shrimp
6 green onions, chopped
2 tbsp olive oil
½ c slivered almonds
2 cans minced clams

¾ c uncooked shell macaroni
2 tbsp tomato paste
2 c chicken stock
1 c V-8 juice
½ c cooked frozen peas
½ c cooked diced celery

Poach the shrimp for 4 minutes. Shell, clean and cut in half. Sauté the green onions in the olive oil in a large soup kettle until soft, about 10 minutes. Add the shrimp, almonds and ham. Mix well and cook for 4 minutes. Drain the clams, reserving the liquid. Mix the macaroni, tomato paste, and the reserved clam juice together in a separate saucepan. Add the chicken stock and V-8 juice and simmer for 8 minutes. Add the peas, clams and celery and pour into the shrimp mixture. Mix thoroughly.

Serves 6.

Jeanne Marie Bonus,
Tyee

Clam Chowder

1 lb bacon
3 medium-size onions, diced
½ c chopped celery
2 large potatoes, diced

1 (12-oz) can clams, chopped
1½ c clam juice
1 pt sour cream
Salt and pepper to taste

Fry the bacon in a skillet. Add the onions and celery. Cover and simmer until the onions and celery are tender. In a separate 5-qt kettle, cover the potatoes with water. Cook until they are almost done, about 10 minutes. Add the clams, clam juice, onions, celery, and bacon. When the potatoes are tender, add the sour cream. Stir and simmer for 5 minutes more. Season with salt and pepper.

Makes 1 qt.

Joanna Norton,
Athlete

Seafood Chowder

6 oz fresh, frozen or canned
  Alaska King crab
1 (4½-oz) can shrimp
1 (8-oz) can minced clams
4 strips bacon, diced
1 clove garlic, minced
2 c diced potatoes
1 c dry white wine
2 tsp salt

Dash of pepper
½ tsp thyme
1 (16-oz) can cream-style
  corn
3 c milk
1 c half-and-half
½ c chopped green onion
2 tbsp minced parsley

Drain the seafoods, reserving any liquid. Slice the crab. In a large saucepan, sauté the bacon and garlic until the bacon is crisp. Add the potatoes, reserved seafood liquid, wine and seasonings. Cover and simmer for 15-20 minutes or until the potatoes are tender. Add the seafoods, corn, milk, half-and-half, onion, and parsley. Heat slowly to simmer, but do not boil.

Serves 6-8.

Joan (Mrs. Robert G.) Waldo,
Vice Provost's wife

Julia Child's Vichyssoise

3 c peeled, sliced potatoes
3 c sliced white of leeks
1½ qt white stock, chicken
stock, or canned chicken broth

½ to 1 c whipping cream
Salt to taste
White pepper
2 to 3 tbsp minced chives

Simmer the vegetables in the stock or broth in a 3-4 qt saucepan, partially covered, for 40-50 minutes, until the vegetables are tender. Or cook the vegetables in a pressure cooker under 15 lb pressure, then simmer in the stock, uncovered for 15 minutes. Purée the soup in an electric blender. Stir in the cream, then season the soup to taste. Chill. Serve the soup in chilled soup cups and decorate with the minced chives.

Serves 6-8.

Jackie Henry,
Athlete

Hearty Beef and Vegetable Soup

2 lb shin of beef
1 large marrow bone
3 tbsp salt
1 gallon water
4 c thinly sliced cabbage
  (approx 1-lb)
1½ c chopped onion
6 carrots, cut in 3" pieces
¾ c chopped green pepper
1 (1-lb 12-oz) can tomatoes,
  undrained
1 (10-oz) pkg frozen lima beans

1 (9-oz) pkg frozen cut green
  beans
1 (10-oz) pkg frozen peas
1 (12-oz) can whole-kernel
  corn, drained
1 potato, skinned and cubed
2 tbsp chopped parsley
1 (6-oz) can tomato paste
½ tsp ground cloves
1 tsp sugar
½ tsp pepper

Place the beef, bone, 1 tbsp salt, and water in a large kettle. Cover and bring to a boil, then skim the surface of any grease. Add the cabbage, onion, carrots, celery, green pepper, and tomatoes. Bring to a boil again, then simmer, covered, for 30 minutes. Add the lima beans, green beans, peas, corn, potato, parsley, tomato paste, cloves, sugar, remaining 2 tbsp salt, and pepper. Simmer, covered, for 3½ hours. Remove the meat and any marrow from the bone, then discard the bone. Let the meat cool, then cut it into cubes and add it to the soup. Refrigerate overnight. Remove any grease from the surface of the soup. Before serving, slowly heat the soup to boiling.

Makes 6½ qt.

Jeb Best,
Athlete

Black Bean Soup

1 pt black beans
2 tbsp chopped onion
1 clove garlic, minced
¼ c fat or butter
1 celery root, diced
2 qt cold water

2 tsp salt
¼ tsp freshly ground pepper
Dash of cayenne pepper
¼ tsp dry mustard
1 lemon, thinly sliced

Wash the beans and soak them overnight in water. Drain, then rinse. Sauté the onion and garlic in the fat or butter until soft. Add to the beans with the celery root and the water. Cook over low heat until the beans are soft. Add boiling water if necessary. Push the beans through a sieve, then season with salt, pepper, cayenne to taste, and mustard. Garnish with the lemon slices.

Serves 6-8.

Bob MacDonald,
Coaching Staff

Baked Minestrone Soup

1 ½ lb lean stew meat
1 c chopped onion
1 tsp minced garlic
1 tsp salt
¼ tsp pepper
2 tbsp olive oil
3 (10½-oz) cans beef broth
2 cans water
1 ½ tsp Italian seasoning

1 (1-lb) can tomatoes, undrained
1 (15¼-oz) can kidney beans
1¾ c ripe olives, reserving 1 c liquid
1 ½ c thinly sliced carrots
1 c small sea shell macaroni
2 c thinly sliced zucchini
Grated Parmesan cheese

Cut the beef into 1¼" cubes. Mix the beef, onion, garlic, salt, and pepper in a dutch oven. Add the olive oil, stirring to coat the meat evenly. Brown, uncovered, in a preheated 400° oven for about 40 minutes, stirring once or twice. Reduce the heat to 350°. Add the broth, water, and Italian seasonings. Cover and cook for 1 hour, until the meat is almost tender. Remove from the oven and stir in the tomatoes, kidney beans, ripe olives, olive liquid, carrots, and macaroni. Sprinkle the zucchini on top. Cover and return to the oven to bake for 40-45 minutes until the macaroni is tender. Serve with grated Parmesan cheese.

Makes about 3½ qts,
Serves 8.

Jimmy Mora,
Athlete

Minestrone Soup

1½ lb lean hamburger
1 large onion, chopped
1 (28-oz) can whole
  tomatoes, chopped
6 beef bouillon cubes
1½ qt water
2 tsp basil
2 tsp oregano
1 tsp garlic salt
1 (20-oz) pkg frozen Italian
  vegetables

2 small zucchini, sliced
  ¼" thick
½ c red wine
1 c macaroni
2 (15¼-oz) cans kidney beans
2 bay leaves
1 (46-oz) can tomato juice
Grated Parmesan cheese

Crumble and brown the hamburger in an 8-qt soup kettle. Drain off any excess fat. Add the onion and tomatoes, then the bouillon cubes, water, basil, oregano, and garlic salt. Simmer for 10 minutes. Add the frozen vegetables and simmer for 5 minutes more. Add the zucchini, red wine, macaroni, kidney beans, bay leaves, and tomato juice. Simmer for 30 minutes or longer. Serve with grated Parmesan cheese sprinkled on top.

Serves 10-12.

Lorraine Stromswold,
Tyee

Tomato Soup

3 qt sliced ripe tomatoes
6 onions, thinly sliced
8 tbsp sugar
Few springs of parsley
40 whole cloves
4 tsp salt

½ tsp pepper
6 tbsp butter
6 tbsp cornstarch
½ c water
Whipped cream

Boil the tomatoes, onions, sugar, parsley, cloves, salt and pepper until the vegetables are thoroughly cooked. Strain the mixture, then add the butter. Add the cornstarch dissolved with the water. Boil until the soup is slightly thickened. Serve the soup hot with a tbsp of whipped cream for each serving.

Makes 5 qt.

Rick Brown,
Athlete

Pozole Soup

2 large fresh pork hocks, each
  cut in 2 or 3 pieces
2 qt water
1 (1-lb) can tomatoes
2 (1-lb) cans hominy, drained

2 medium-size onions, finely
  chopped
4 tsp salt
Chopped fresh vegetables
  and cheese (see below)
2 limes, cut in wedges

Place the pork hocks into a large kettle with the water, tomatoes, hominy, onions, and salt. Simmer for 2 to 3 hours, or until the meat begins to come away from the bones. Remove the pork hocks from the soup and cool both the meat and soup. Remove the meat from the hocks, discarding any fat and bones; cut the meat into small pieces. When the soup is cold, skim off any excess grease. Just before serving, add the meat to the soup and heat, seasoning with salt. To serve, sprinkle an assortment of fresh vegetables into the soup. For example, shredded lettuce, chopped radishes, thinly sliced green onions, shredded carrots, chopped avocado and cubes of cream cheese all go well. Serve lime wedges on the side.

Serves 6.

Mary Gates,
Tyee

Oxtail Soup

2½ lb lean oxtails, chopped
4½ qt water
1 (8-oz) can whole tomatoes
2 stalks celery, diced
1 large onion, chopped
1 tbsp whole allspice

1 tbsp salt
1 tbsp chopped parsley
1 bay leaf
2 large carrots, sliced
½ c pearl barley (optional)
Hot cooked noodles

In a large kettle, gently boil the oxtails in the water, uncovered, for 1 hour. Skim any grease off the surface carefully. Add the tomatoes, celery, onion, allspice, salt, parsley, and bay leaf and simmer, uncovered, for 1½ hours. Add the carrots and barley, then cover and cook until tender, about 1 hour. Serve poured over the noodles into bowls. This soup may be frozen.

Makes 2 qt.

Vince Albritton,
Athlete

Washington Dog Breath Chili

1½ medium-size onions,
  chopped
1 green pepper, chopped
2 stalks celery, chopped
3 lb lean hamburger
1 lb sirloin, cubed
3 cloves garlic, minced
3 fresh hot green or yellow
  chili peppers

1 (6-oz) can tomato paste
1 (16-oz) can stewed tomatoes
1 (15-oz) can tomato sauce
1 (7-oz) can chili salsa
½ can beer
3 oz chili powder
Pepper and oregano
Salt and garlic salt to taste

Cook, the onion, green pepper and celery in enough oil to cover the bottom of a soup kettle. Add the meat and brown, cooking about 15 minutes. Remove any excess grease. Add all the remaining ingredients, sprinkling the pepper and oregano to cover the top of the stew. Simmer 2½ hours, stirring every 15-20 minutes.

Serves 8-10.

Chuck Schluter,
Tyee

Cream of Avocado Soup

2 ripe avocados
¼ c plain yogurt
½ c beef consommé
1 tbsp chopped onion
1 tsp diced green chilies
½ clove garlic, minced
1½ tsp lemon juice

2 c half-and-half
Hot pepper sauce
Worcestershire sauce
Salt and pepper
Shrimp
Parsley

Combine the avocados, yogurt, consommé, onion, chilies, garlic, and lemon juice in a blender container. Blend until smooth and creamy. Pour the avocado mixture into a mixing bowl. Mix in enough half-and-half to achieve a creamy consistency. Add the hot pepper sauce, Worcestershire and salt and pepper to taste. Cover and refrigerate until well chilled. Serve with a garnish of shrimp and a sprig of parsley.

Makes 3½ c.

Ruth (Mrs. William) Gerberding,
President's wife

Broccoli Soup

2 pkg frozen chopped broccoli
¼ c chopped onion
2 c chicken broth
2 tbsp butter
1 tbsp flour

1 tsp salt
⅛ tsp mace
Dash of pepper
2 c half-and-half

Combine the broccoli, onion, and chicken broth and simmer for 10 minutes. Place the mixture in the blender and blend until smooth. Melt the butter, then add the flour, salt, mace, and pepper, stirring until smooth. Slowly pour the half-and-half into the flour mixture, then add the broccoli mixture. Heat to a boiling point.

Serves 8.

Sue Silberman,
Tyee

Portuguese Bean Soup

A good "keeper" that freezes well.

1 lb dry kidney beans
2½ qt cold water
½ onion, minced
1 stalk celery, minced
1 lb smoked ham shank
1 (6-oz.) can tomato paste

1 large potato, diced
1 small carrot, minced
1 (7 oz.) hot spiced
   Portuguese sausage
Salt and pepper to taste

Rinse the beans well. Cover with the water and boil for ½ hour. Add the minced onion and celery. Reduce the heat to medium and add the smoked ham shank and simmer for 1 hour. Remove the meat from the bone in pieces by stirring slowly, then discard the bone. Add tomato paste and water as needed. Then add the potato and carrot and gently boil the soup for ½ hour. Cut the sausage in pieces and add it to the soup. Cook for 1½ hours on medium heat. Season with salt and pepper to taste and simmer at the lowest heat until serving time.

Serves 6.

Janie (Mrs. Alan) Kutz,
Tyee

Herbed Onion and Tomato Soup

This soup is almost as good as a win over USC!

3 c onions, finely chopped
½ c olive oil
3 large tomatoes, peeled,
  seeded, and chopped
3 tbsp fresh basil, chopped

3 tbsp fresh parsley, chopped
3 cloves garlic, minced
1 ½ qt chicken stock
6 eggs, soft poached
6 toasted bread triangles

Sauté the onions in the olive oil over low heat, stirring frequently, for 20 minutes or until they are tender. Add the tomatoes, basil, parsley, and garlic and cook the mixture for 2 minutes. Add the chicken stock and simmer the soup for 20 minutes, seasoning with salt if necessary. Divide the soup into 6 bowls and drop a soft poached egg into each one. Garnish the soup with toasted bread triangles.

Serves 6.

Pat Zakskorn,
Athlete

Chilled Lime and Honeydew Soup

1 honeydew melon
½ c lime juice
½ c chicken broth
¼ c sour cream
1 ½ tbsp preserved ginger,
  minced

3 tbsp ginger syrup
1 lime, thinly sliced
Dash of freshly grated
  nutmeg
Dash of sweet paprika

Peel, seed, and chop the melon. In a glass bowl, combine the melon with the lime juice. Cover the mixture and chill for 1 hour. In a blender, purée the melon mixture. Add the chicken broth, sour cream, minced ginger, and ginger syrup. Purée the mixture until it is well combined. Transfer the soup to a bowl and chill it, covered, for 30 minutes or longer. Ladle the soup into chilled bowls and garnish each serving with thin lime slices, freshly grated nutmeg and sweet paprika.

Preserved ginger is available at specialty food stores and some supermarkets.

Serves 6.

Shirlee Humphrey Liberman,
Tyee

Pumpkin Soup

Excellent with fowl or game.

1 large white onion,
  finely chopped
½ c butter
1 (29-oz) can solid pack
  pumpkin
1 can chicken broth

Pinch of powdered ginger
Pinch of cayenne
½ pt heavy cream
Parsley
Watercress

Sauté the onion in the butter in a soup pan. Add the pumpkin and chicken broth and simmer. Cool the pumpkin mixture, then whip it in a blender until smooth. Pour it back into the saucepan and add the powdered ginger and cayenne. Add the heavy cream and simmer for 10 minutes. Sprinkle fresh watercress or parsley on top of each bowl before serving.

Serves 6.

Leslie Walker,
Tyee

Gazpacho

4 c tomato juice, chilled
1 small onion, minced
2 c diced tomatoes
1 c minced green pepper
1 tsp honey
1 cucumber, diced
2 scallions, chopped
Salt and black pepper to taste
Juice of ½ lemon and 1 lime

2 tbsp wine vinegar
1 tsp tarragon
1 tsp basil
1 clove garlic, crushed
Dash of ground cumin
¼ c chopped parsley
Dash of Tabasco sauce
2 tbsp olive oil

Combine all the ingredients, mixing thoroughly. Chill for at least 2 hours.

Serves 6.

Sheilah Collins,
Athlete

Chicken-Ball Soup

Chicken Balls:
1 c ground raw chicken
  (approx. ½ lb boned
  chicken breast)
2 tbsp chopped parsley
1 tbsp grated Parmesan cheese
½ c bread crumbs
¼ tsp salt
¼ tsp pepper
2 egg whites

Soup:
2 tbsp olive or salad oil
1 c sliced mushrooms
1 c sliced green onion
1 tbsp lemon juice
½ tsp salt
¼ tsp dried oregano leaves
¼ tsp pepper
4 (13¾-oz) cans chicken
  broth
1 c spaghetti, broken
Parsley
Parmesan cheese

For the chicken balls: In a medium-size bowl, combine the ground chicken with the parsley, cheese, bread crumbs, ¼ tsp salt, pepper, and egg whites. Refrigerate, covered, for 1 hour or until firm. Shape the mixture in 1" balls and refrigerate.

For the soup: In a 6-qt dutch oven, sauté the mushrooms and onion in the oil for about 3 minutes. Add the lemon juice, ½ tsp salt, oregano, and ¼ tsp pepper and mix well. Stir in the chicken broth and bring the mixture to a boil. Gradually add the chicken balls and spaghetti. Cook, stirring occasionally, until the chicken balls are done, about 10 minutes. Garnish with chopped parsley and Parmesan cheese.

Makes 2½ qt.

Bernie Jackson,
Athlete

SALADS

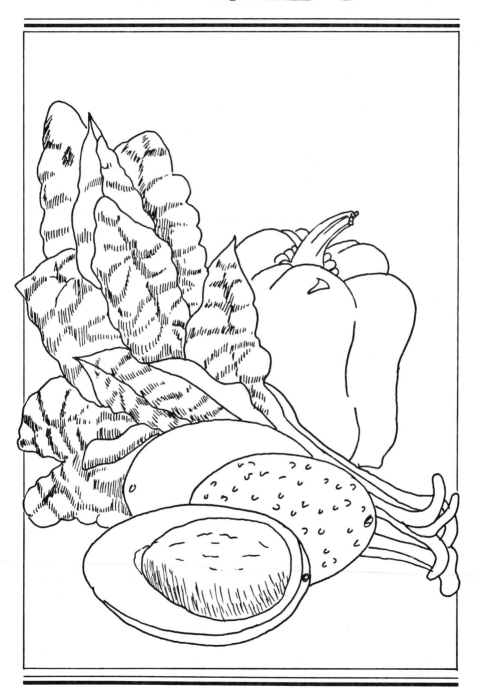

Vernell Mint Frozen Salad

1 (10-oz) pkg miniature
  marshmallows
2 (1-lb 13-oz) cans crushed
  pineapple
2 tbsp lemon juice
1 (3-oz) pkg lime gelatin

1 pt whipping cream, beaten
1 pkg Vernell butter mints,
  crushed
1 tsp pineapple flavoring
1 tsp mint flavoring

Mix together the marshmallow, pineapple and lemon juice. Sprinkle the gelatin over the mixture and refrigerate overnight. Fold in the whipped cream, mints and flavorings. Pour the mixture into ice trays or into 1 large glass pan, and freeze. This dessert keeps well in the freezer for months.

Dorothy (Mrs. Marv) Harshman,
Coaching Staff

Grandma James' Holiday Salad

1 jar pimiento cheese
1 medium-size carton Cool
  Whip

1 can crushed pineapple,
  drained
½ bag miniature
  marshmallows

Mix together the cheese and the Cool Whip. Add the pineapple and the marshmallows. Freeze in an 8"x8" glass pan. Serve on a bed of lettuce and top with a cherry.

Serves 8.

Jill Woodruff,
Coaching Staff

Rainbow Salad

1 large can fruit cocktail
1 large can crushed pineapple
3 pkg lemon gelatin
2 (3-oz) pkg cream cheese

1 small jar pimiento
½ c chopped celery
⅔ c chopped nuts
½ pt whipping cream, beaten

Drain the fruit, retaining the syrup. Add enough water to the syrup to make 5½ c liquid,

Serves 15.

Marilyn Head,
Tyee

Peach Salad

1 large can sliced peaches,
  drained and diced
1 c miniature marshmallows
½ c maraschino cherries,
  chopped
1 large banana, sliced

¼ c chopped nuts

Dressing:
1 c Cool Whip
⅓ c Miracle Whip
1 tbsp lemon juice

Mix the dressing ingredients, then toss in a large bowl with the fruits and marshmallows. Chill.

Serves 6.

Karen Dorr,
Coaching Staff

Chinese Fruit Bowl

1 ripe pineapple (approx. 3 lb)
1 pt strawberries, washed
  and hulled
1 (11-oz) can litchi nuts,
  drained
1 (11-oz) can mandarin
  oranges, drained

½ c preserved whole
  kumquats
2 bananas, sliced diagonally
½ c syrup from the kumquats
¾ c white rum
2 tbsp chopped candied
  ginger

Remove the pineapple from the shell, core and slice into bite-size chunks. Gently toss the pineapple with all the remaining ingredients. Refrigerate, covered, until well chilled, 2 hours or longer.

Serves 12–14.

Sue Kruszewski,
Coaching Staff

Frozen Cherry Bombe Salad

1 (16-oz) can dark or light
   sweet cherries
½ c cherry syrup
1½ tsp unflavored gelatin
5 tbsp mayonnaise
1 c whipping cream

2 tbsp powdered sugar
1 (11-oz) can mandarin
   oranges, drained
1 (3-oz) pkg cream cheese
½ c miniature marshmallows
3 tbsp chopped pecans

Drain the cherries, reserving the syrup; halve them and remove the pits, then set aside. Soften the gelatin in ½ c cherry syrup, then heat until dissolved. Stir in 3 tbsp mayonnaise and let the mixture cool. Whip the cream. Reserve ½ c for filling; fold remainder into the gelatin mixture, along with the cherries, 1 tbsp sugar and the oranges. Pour the mixture into a 1-qt mold. Place a 10-oz custard cup in the center of the mold and a weight in the cup to make an indentation for the filling. Freeze the mold until almost firm, then remove the custard cup. Combine the cream cheese with the remaining 2 tbsp mayonnaise. Fold in the reserved whipped cream, marshmallows and nuts. Pour the mixture into the center of the mold. Freeze overnight or until firm. Before serving, unmold and let stand in the refrigerator for 20 minutes, then cut into wedges.

Serves 6–8.

Ellen Pottmeyer,
Athlete

Five Cup Fruit Salad

1 c drained mandarin oranges
1 c drained pineapple chunks
1 c sour cream

1 c miniature marshmallows
1 c coconut

Combine all the ingredients and chill for 8 hours or overnight.

Serves 6.

Ron Forsell,
News Media

Grapefruit Curry Salad

1 (7-oz) can, or 1 c diced,
  cooked tuna, chicken or ham
½ c finely diced celery
¼ c slivered ripe olives

¼ c mayonnaise
½ tsp curry powder
2 c grapefruit sections

Combine the tuna, ham or chicken with the celery and ripe olives. Blend together the mayonnaise and curry. Add the mayonnaise mixture to the meat and toss lightly. Add the grapefruit and toss lightly again. Serve the salad on greens.

Serves 4.

Laurie Coaston,
Athlete

Frosted Cranberry Squares

2 (3-oz) pkgs strawberry
  gelatin
1½ c boiling water
1 (1-lb) can whole cranberry
  sauce
1½ c ginger ale
1 c chopped walnuts
1 c chopped unpared apple

1 (8½-oz) can crushed
  pineapple, drained
1 small banana, diced
1 tbsp grated orange rind
1 c heavy cream
1 (3-oz) pkg cream cheese,
  softened

Dissolve the gelatin in the boiling water. Add the cranberry sauce, stirring until dissolved. Stir in the ginger ale and chill until thick and syrupy. Fold in the walnuts, apple, pineapple, banana and orange rind. Pour the mixture into a lightly-oiled 8"x8" baking dish. Chill until set. Combine the heavy cream and cream cheese. Beat until the cream is whipped and the mixture is thick. Spread over the gelatin. Chill for at least 1 hour. To serve, cut in squares.

Serves 9.

Jan Harville,
Coaching Staff

Avocado and Artichoke Salad

Salad:
1 ripe avocado
Lettuce, torn
1 (14-oz) can artichoke
  hearts
Capers

Dressing:
¼ tsp minced garlic
½ tsp salt
¼ c lemon juice
¼ c olive oil
1 tsp dill
¼ tsp pepper

Mash the garlic with the salt until smooth. Place in a jar with the lemon juice and shake. Add the oil, dill and pepper and shake again. Peel and cut the avocado into chunks and mix with the torn lettuce leaves. Drain the artichoke hearts, cut them into quarters and add to the avocados. Pour the dressing over and sprinkle with capers.

Serves 8.

Mary C. Foster,
Administrative Staff

Wine-Marinated Mushroom and Olive Salad

Serve as an hors d'oeuvre, or in a tossed green salad with vinegar and oil dressing.

20 medium-size mushrooms,
  trimmed and halved
1 (15-oz) can pitted black
  olives
2 red onions, cut in rings
¼ c chopped parsley
1 c olive oil

½ c dry white wine
¼ c lemon juice
1 clove garlic, crushed
1 tsp salt
¼ tsp pepper
1 tsp oregano

In a bowl, mix the mushrooms, olives, onions and parsley. In a separate bowl, combine the remaining ingredients and beat until smooth. The marinade will thicken slightly. Pour the marinade over the mushrooms, olives, onions and parsley, stirring to coat well. Cover and marinate overnight or for several days. If to be used in a salad, strain the vegetables first. The oil/wine mixture may be saved and reused.

Doris Alexander,
Tyee

Olive Wreath Mold

1 (3-oz) pkg lime gelatin
1 c boiling water
⅔ c cold water
2 tbsp lemon juice
1 c heavy cream, whipped
⅓ c sliced pimiento-stuffed
   olives plus 24 slices

½ c grated American cheese
1 (8-oz) can crushed
   pineapple, drained
½ pimiento, chopped
½ c finely chopped celery
½ c chopped walnuts
½ tsp salt

Dissolve the gelatin in the boiling water. Add the cold water and lemon juice, then chill until thick and syrupy. Fold in the whipped cream. Add the ⅓ c sliced olives, cheese, pineapple, pimiento, celery, walnuts and salt, blending thoroughly. Arrange the 24 olive slices in a circle around the bottom of a greased 9" ring mold. Pour the mixture into the mold. Chill until set.

Serves 6–8.

Marius Felix,
Athlete

Tomato Aspic

2¼ c tomato juice
1 small bay leaf
4 cloves
2 slices of onion
3 slices of lemon
1 pkg lemon jello

1 tsp salt
⅛ tsp white pepper
¼ c diced celery
¼ c sliced ripe olives
½ c small shrimp

Bring the tomato juice, bay leaf, cloves, onion and lemon to a boil. Simmer for 15 minutes. Strain, then add the gelatin to the hot liquid, stirring to dissolve. Add the salt and white pepper. When partially thickened, add the celery, olives and shrimp. Pour into a 1-qt mold and refrigerate until set.

Serves 6.

Mrs. Charles P. Moriarty,
Tyee

Layered Vegetable Salad

1 medium-size head of
 lettuce, shredded
1 pkg frozen peas
1 c chopped celery
8 slices bacon, fried and
 crumbled
Chopped green onion to taste

1 can sliced water chestnuts
4 hard-cooked eggs, sliced
Uncle Dan's Salad Dressing or
 Ranch Style Dressing
½ lb Cheddar cheese, grated
2 medium-size tomatoes,
 sliced

Layer the shredded lettuce, uncooked frozen peas, chopped celery, crumbled bacon, green onion and sliced water chestnuts in a cake pan. Lay the sliced egg on top. Cover with Uncle Dan's or Ranch Style dressing. Sprinkle grated cheese on the top and decorate with sliced tomatoes. Chill.

Serves 10.

Jeanne Grainger,
Administrative Staff

Spinach Salad

Salad:
1 lb fresh spinach
1 c bean sprouts
1 c boiling water
1 c fresh mushrooms
½ small can water chestnuts
1½ tbsp toasted sesame
 seeds

Dressing:
½ c oil
¼ c soy sauce
2 tbsp lemon juice
½ tsp sugar
½ tsp pepper
1½ tbsp minced onion

For the salad: Clean, drain and tear the spinach, then chill. Cover the bean sprouts with the boiling water. Let stand for 5 minutes, then drain and cool. Cut the mushrooms and water chestnuts into thin slices. Mix the vegetables together, then refrigerate. Pour the dressing over the salad just before serving and top with toasted sesame seeds. To toast the sesame seeds, place them on a tray in a 300° oven for 10 minutes.

For the dressing: Mix all the ingredients together in a jar and shake well. Refrigerate.

Serves 6–8.

Margaret Cordell,
Tyee

Caesar Salad

1 c peanut oil
1 clove garlic, crushed
2 c bread cubes
2 heads romaine lettuce
1 head Bibb lettuce
1 bunch watercress
¾ c grated Parmesan cheese

½ tsp salt
¼ tsp dry mustard
¼ tsp black pepper
⅓ c lemon juice
2 eggs, lightly beaten
Dash of Worcestershire sauce
1 (2-oz) can anchovy filets

Pour the peanut oil into a jar. Add the crushed garlic and cover. Let stand for at least 1 hour. Using ¼ of this oil, sauté the bread cubes until golden brown. Tear the romaine, Bibb and watercress into a large salad bowl. Sprinkle with the Parmesan cheese, salt, dry mustard and black pepper. Pour on the remaining ¾ c oil, and the lemon juice and eggs. Add the Worcestershire, anchovy filets and croutons. Toss lightly until well mixed.

Serves 10–12.

David Whitennight,
Athlete

Marinated Vegetable Salad

2 pkg frozen broccoli spears
1 pkg frozen asparagus
1 can or pkg green beans
1 can artichoke hearts, halved

Marinade:
½ c light cream
2 tbsp lemon juice
2 tbsp vinegar
1 c mayonnaise
1 tbsp chopped parsley
2 tbsp chopped onion
3 tbsp chopped cucumber
Salt to taste

Cook the vegetables until tender and cool quickly. Arrange on a platter in spoke fashion. Mix together all the ingredients for the marinade and pour over the vegetables. Refrigerate for at least 6 hours.

Serves 6–8.

Kay Larson,
Tyee

Scallop Salad

1 lb fresh scallops
1 c beer
½ c flour
3 tbsp butter
⅓ c and 3 tbsp olive oil
1½ tsp crushed garlic

3 tbsp chopped parsley
1 lb potatoes
Salt and pepper to taste
½ lemon, rind and juice
½ c sour cream
¼ c chopped dill pickle

Wash and dry the scallops. Dip in the beer and then in the flour. Sauté in the butter and 3 tbsp olive oil very quickly, adding the garlic and parsley when almost done. Cool. Boil the potatoes in salted water. Peel them while they are still hot and slice into a bowl. Add the ⅓ c olive oil and let cool. Add salt and pepper to taste, then the lemon rind and juice and the sour cream. Turn the potatoes several times, adding more lemon if desired. Add the scallops and dill pickle. Serve on a bed of lettuce.

Serves 6–8.

Vera Klein
Tyee

Crab Mold

1 (8-oz) pkg cream cheese
1 can cream of mushroom
   soup
1 can crab meat
1 pkg Knox unflavored gelatin

¼ c cold water
1 c finely chopped celery
1 bunch green onions,
   chopped
1 c mayonnaise

Heat the cream cheese and mushroom soup until well mixed. Dissolve the gelatin in the cold water, and add to the cream cheese mixture immediately. Add the remaining ingredients and pour into a small mold. Refrigerate overnight.

Serves 6.

Betty (Mrs. Richard A.) Smith,
Tyee

Green Goddess Salad

Dressing:
¼ c chopped parsley
¼ c chopped green onions
2 tbsp chopped chives
1 tbsp chopped anchovy
   filets
1 large clove garlic, crushed
1 c mayonnaise
¼ c heavy cream
2 tbsp tarragon vinegar
2 to 3 drops green food coloring

Salad:
6 c shredded romaine lettuce
2 c cooked shrimp, chilled
1 c cooked crab meat or
   lobster

For the dressing: In a bowl, combine the parsley, onions, chives, anchovies, garlic and mayonnaise, mixing thoroughly. Add the cream, vinegar and food coloring. Mix well, then chill.

For the salad: Place the lettuce in a large salad bowl and make a well in the center. Pour the salad dressing into the well and surround with the shrimp and crab meat or lobster.

Serves 6.

Shyril O'Steen,
Athlete

Chicken Salad Supreme in Cantaloupe Shells

4 cantaloupes
5 c diced cooked chicken
1 tsp salt
1 c seedless grapes
1 (5-oz) can roasted, slivered
　almonds

¼ c chopped green onions
1 tsp grated lemon rind
1 c lemon juice
½ c mayonnaise

Halve, peel and dice 1 cantaloupe to make 1½ c diced melon. In a large bowl, sprinkle the chicken with the salt and mix well. Add the diced cantaloupe, grapes, almonds, onions and lemon rind. Sprinkle with the lemon juice and mix gently. Cover the mixture and refrigerate. Cut the remaining 3 cantaloupes into halves and scrape out the seeds and pulp. Fold the mayonnaise into the chicken mixture, then spoon into the melon halves.

Serves 6.

Jane McDougall,
Athlete

Spinach Salad

Salad:
2 lb fresh spinach
2 heads red leaf lettuce or
　1 head iceberg lettuce
½ lb bacon, fried and
　crumbled

Dressing:
¼ c sugar
1 tsp salt
1 tsp dry mustard
1 tbsp onion juice
⅓ c cider vinegar
1 c salad oil
1 tbsp poppy seeds
1½ c large-curd cottage
　cheese

Tear the spinach into large pieces and add bite-size pieces of lettuce, then the crumbled bacon. Combine the sugar, salt, mustard, onion juice, vinegar and oil in a jar and shake. Add the poppy seeds and shake again. Pour ½ the dressing over the greens. Add the cottage cheese to the remaining dressing, shake well, and pour over the salad.

Serves 8.

Robert F. Philip,
Tyee

Garlic Dressing

⅔ c olive or vegetable oil
⅓ c red wine vinegar
3 cloves garlic, crushed
1 tsp mixed Italian herbs,
   crumbled

1 tsp salt
¼ tsp freshly ground pepper

Combine the oil, vinegar, garlic, Italian herbs, salt and pepper in a 2-c jar. Cover the jar and shake to blend well.

Makes 1 c.

Gil Gamble,
Coaching Staff

Roquefort Cheese Dressing

1 tsp salt
⅛ tsp paprika
½ lb Roquefort cheese,
   crumbled

½ c small-curd cottage
   cheese
2 tbsp olive oil
1 c sour cream

Beat all the ingredients together until almost smooth.

Makes 1 pt.

Brunno DeFeo,
Athlete

Honey Dressing

Excellent for fruit.

⅔ c sugar
1 tsp dry mustard
1 tsp paprika
¼ tsp salt
5 tbsp vinegar

1 tbsp lemon juice
1 tsp grated onion
1 tsp celery seed
⅓ c honey
1 c salad oil

Combine all the ingredients except the oil. Slowly add the oil, beating the mixture with an electric mixer. Store the dressing in the refrigerator.

Makes 1 pt.

Janet R. Koplowitz,
Tyee

CASSEROLES
&
SANDWICHES

Triple-Decker Seafood Sandwich

12 slices thin white bread,
 crusts removed
Mayonnaise
4 slices tomato
Egg Salad:
6 eggs, hard-cooked and
 mashed
Salt and pepper to taste
½ tsp Grey Poupon mustard
4 tbsp mayonnaise

Sauce:
¾ c mayonnaise
½ c pimiento
Juice of 1 lemon
1 tsp onion juice
2 cans crab or shrimp

For each sandwich, spread 1 slice of bread with the mayonnaise and top with a tomato slice. Spread the second slice with egg salad and the third with the seafood sauce. Stack the slices, spread side up.

Serves 4.

Dorothy (Mrs. Marv) Harshman,
Coaching Staff

Luncheon Sandwich

12 slices thin white bread
1 (8-oz) pkg cream cheese
½ c chopped green onion
½ c crisp chopped bacon
6 tomato slices

1 c crab or shrimp
½ c Thousand Island dressing
 or
¼ c mayonnaise mixed with
 ¼ c chili sauce

Cut the bread into 2½" rounds. On 6 rounds, spread cream cheese, then top with onions and bacon. On the remaining 6 rounds, place a slice of tomato, then the crab or shrimp. Stack the tomato-covered round on the cheese-covered round and top with Thousand Island dressing or mayonnaise/chili sauce.

Serves 6.

Dorothy (Mrs. Marv) Harshman,
Coaching Staff

Broiled Crab Sandwich

1 c crab, fresh, frozen or
   canned
1 c mayonnaise

1 c chili sauce
1 ½ c grated Cheddar cheese
6 hamburger buns

Mix the crab, mayonnaise, chili sauce and 1 c cheese together. Refrigerate for about 12 hours to let the flavors blend. Spread the mixture on the bottom half of the hamburger buns and sprinkle with the remaining cheese. Broil slowly on the center rack of the oven until bubbly. Serve at once, either open-faced or closed with the other ½ of the hamburger bun.

Serves 6.

Dorothy (Mrs. Marv) Harshman,
Coaching Staff

Hot Crab Sandwich

1 c crab
1 c shrimp
1 c sour cream
1 c Parmesan cheese
1 c mayonnaise

4 English muffins
4 slices red onion or
¼ c chopped green onion
4 slices tomato

Combine the crab, shrimp, sour cream, cheese, and mayonnaise; mix thoroughly. Spread the mixture on an english muffin and top with the onion and tomato. Bake the sandwich at 350° for 15 minutes, or until bubbly. The filling may be made ahead and refrigerated. Remove it 1 hour before assembling the sandwiches.

Serves 4.

Dorothy (Mrs. Marv) Harshman,
Coaching Staff

Corned Beef Casserole

2 cans corned beef hash
2 c grated cheese
8 hard-cooked eggs, diced
1 c crushed potato chips

Sauce:
¼ c butter
½ c flour
4 c milk
½ tsp salt (or celery or onion
  salt)
⅛ tsp pepper
1 tsp Worcestershire sauce

Spread the corned beef in a buttered 9" x 13" casserole. Cover it with the grated cheese and the eggs. Pour the sauce over the casserole evenly and refrigerate overnight. Sprinkle it with the potato chips and bake at 350° for 45 minutes.

For the sauce: In a medium-size saucepan, melt the butter. Add the flour, stirring constantly. Add the milk, 1 c at a time, continuing to stir. Cook the sauce until it begins to thicken. Add the salt, pepper and Worcestershire sauce.

Hazel (Mrs. G. M.) Whitacre,
Tyee

Lucibelle's Baked Beans

3 c navy beans
½ c molasses
½ c brown sugar
¼ c vinegar
¼ c ketchup
Salt to taste

¼ tsp pepper
Dash of Tabasco sauce
1 onion, chopped
½ c chopped green pepper
1 pkg ham hocks

Soak the beans overnight in 1 qt of water. Drain, then cover the beans with water and cook for 1 hour. Combine all the ingredients and bake in a covered pot at 250° for 8 hours. Stir the beans every hour or so, adding water if they get dry.

Serves 8.

Rosemary (Mrs. Patrick T.)
Easter, Tyee

Pasta with Mushroom and Zucchini Topping

6 tbsp butter
3 cloves garlic, minced
1 lb mushrooms, sliced
2 tbsp fresh lemon juice
4 small unpeeled zucchini,
  cut into 1/4" julienne slices

4 tbsp minced parsley
1 to 2 tsp dried basil
1 1/2 tsp salt
1/8 tsp freshly ground pepper
1 lb freshly cooked pasta,
  preferably homemade

Melt 2 tbsp butter in a large skillet over medium heat. Add 1 garlic clove and cook for 3 minutes. Add the mushrooms and lemon juice and toss until well combined. Add the zucchini, 2 tbsp parsley, basil and salt and blend thoroughly. Cover, increase the heat to medium-high and cook until the vegetables are steamed through, about 3-5 minutes, shaking the pan frequently. Place the remaining butter and garlic in a large serving bowl. Add the hot pasta and the remaining parsley and toss well. Top with vegetables and toss again. Taste and adjust the seasoning.

Serves 6.

Chris James,
Athlete

Marvelous Macaroni and Cheese

2 c elbow macaroni
3 tbsp butter
1/4 c chopped onion
3 tbsp flour
1/2 tsp salt

1/8 tsp pepper
1 c heavy cream
1/2 c dry white wine
2 c grated sharp Cheddar
  cheese

Cook the macaroni according to pkg directions; drain and set aside. Heat the butter and sauté the onion until tender. Stir in the flour, salt, and pepper. Slowly add the cream and wine and cook over low heat, stirring constantly, until thickened. Add the cheese and stir until melted. Mix together the macaroni and cheese sauce. Place in a greased 1 1/2 qt casserole. Bake in a preheated 350° oven for 15 minutes, or until thoroughly heated.

Serves 4-6.

Cricket Marshall,
Athlete

Layers of Hot Stuff

1 large can refried beans
1 can black olives
Dash of Tabasco sauce
1 pt sour cream
1 c each grated Cheddar and
  Monterey Jack cheese
3 tomatoes, chopped
3 green onions, chopped
1 pkg Doritos

Guacamole:
2 avocados, peeled, pitted,
  and mashed
1 medium-size onion,
  finely chopped
2 green chili peppers, finely
  chopped
1 tsp lemon juice
1 tsp salt
½ tsp coarsely ground pepper
½ tsp ascorbic acid mixture
1 medium-size tomato, finely
  chopped

In a large bowl, layer the ingredients in this order: refried beans, ½ the olives, several dashes of Tabasco, sour cream, ½ the cheeses, guacamole, tomatoes, the remaining olives, green onions, several dashes of Tabasco, and top with the remaining cheeses. Cover and refrigerate. Dip with Doritos.

For the guacamole: Mix all the ingredients except the tomato until creamy. Fold in the tomato.

Serves 6.

Lugene St. Cyr,
Administrative Staff

Mexican Casserole

1 lg pkg Doritos, crushed
2 to 3 onions, chopped
3 small cans tomato sauce

2 lb hamburger, browned
and drained
2 cans chili without beans
2 to 3 c grated Cheddar cheese

Layer all the ingredients in a 2 qt casserole as follows: crushed chips, onions, tomato sauce, hamburger, chili, grated cheese. Bake at 350° for 30-45 minutes.

Serves 8.

Catherine (Mrs. Harry E.) Worley, Tyee

Beef Tacos

1 lb hamburger
½ c chopped onion
1 clove garlic, minced
½ tsp salt
½ tsp chili powder
12 tortillas

Shortening
2 tomatos, chopped
3 c finely shredded lettuce
8 oz Cheddar cheese, grated
1 can Mexican hot sauce or
enchilada sauce

In a skillet, cook the hamburger, onion, and garlic until the meat is browned, then drain. Add the salt and chili powder. Set the meat aside and keep warm. In a heavy skillet, fry the tortillas, 1 at a time, in ¼" hot shortening. When the tortilla becomes limp, fold it in half with tongs and hold the edges apart while frying. Fry for 1½-2 minutes or until crisp, then drain. Spoon about ¼ c meat mixture into each. Top with the tomato, lettuce, and cheese and serve with hot sauce.

Serves 6.

Scott Garnett, Athlete

Steak Stroganoff

1 lb round steak, cut
  in ¾" cubes
¼ c flour
2 tbsp fat
½ c chopped onion
1 clove garlic, minced
1 (6-oz) can mushrooms and
  broth

1 c sour cream
1 can cream of mushroom soup
1 tbsp Worcestershire sauce
½ tsp salt
⅛ tsp pepper
2 c cooked rice

Roll the meat in the flour, then brown in hot fat in a large frying pan. Remove the meat, and add the onion, garlic, and mushrooms. Cook gently until the onions are golden. Add the sour cream, Worcestershire, salt and pepper. Cook until thickened and bubbly. Return the meat and simmer, stirring occasionally, for about 1 hour or until the meat is tender. Serve the stroganoff over fluffy cooked rice, topped with Parmesan cheese, if desired.

Serves 4.

Doris and John Ellis,
Tyee

Quick 'n Easy Stroganoff

½ c chopped onions
¼ c butter
1 lb ground beef
2 tbsp flour
½ tsp pepper
1½ tsp salt

½ tsp paprika
1 can cream of chicken soup
1 can sliced water chestnuts
1 can sliced mushrooms
1 c sour cream

In a skillet, sauté the onions in the butter. Mix the meat, flour, pepper, salt and paprika. Add to the onions, cooking until the meat is browned. Add the soup, mushrooms and water chestnuts. Cook for 5 minutes, until warmed thoroughly. Turn off the heat and add the sour cream. Serve the stroganoff over rice or Chinese noodles.

Serves 4.

Carol (Mrs. Don) James,
Coaching Staff

Fasool Ya

Armenian Dish

Rice Pilaf:
½ to 1 c vermicelli or spaghetti
¼ c butter or margarine
1 ½ c long-grain rice
3 c water
1 to 2 tbsp salt

Fasool Ya
1 lb hamburger
½ to 1 whole onion, quartered
Salt and pepper to taste
1 ¼ lb fresh or frozen green beans
1 (28-oz) can whole tomatoes

For the pilaf: Crush the vermicelli into a skillet. Add the butter and brown the vermicelli, then add the rice and brown again. When the rice is brown, add the water and salt to taste. Cover the pan and bring the mixture to a boil. Simmer for approximately 30 minutes.

For the Fasool Ya: Brown the hamburger with the onion, breaking the onion up as you stir. Season with salt and pepper to taste. Once the hamburger is brown, add the canned tomatoes and green beans. Let the mixture simmer until the beans are tender but crisp. Serve the Fasool Ya over the rice pilaf with a generous portion of yogurt.

Serves 4-6.

Vincent Coby,
Athlete

Liberation Stew

3 lb cubed stew meat
8 medium-size onions, quartered
8 carrots, coarsely sliced
6 stalks celery, coarsely sliced
1 (29-oz) can sliced tomatoes
1 tbsp Worcestershire sauce
1 tsp salt
½ tsp pepper
1 tsp dried thyme leaves
3 medium-size potatoes, cut
   into ¾" pieces

2 (4-oz) cans tomato sauce
1 pkg onion soup mix
1 can cream of mushroom soup
2 tsp basil
8 tbsp minute tapioca
1 green onion
¼ c red wine
1 tbsp soy sauce
1 clove garlic, crushed
2 bay leaves

Combine all the ingredients in a large roaster. Cover and bake at 275° for 5 - 6 hours. Stir once or twice while cooking.

Serves 8.

Marilyn Sidel,
Tyee

Beef Casserole

2 lb round steak, cut in 1"
   cubes
3 tbsp flour
½ tsp garlic salt or seasoned
   salt
½ tsp pepper

1 large onion, thinly sliced
½ lb mushrooms, thinly sliced
2 beef bouillon cubes
   dissolved in
1¼ c hot water, and cooled

Place ½ the cubed round steak in a greased deep casserole. Sprinkle with ½ the flour, the salt and pepper. Layer with ½ the onions and ½ the mushrooms. Repeat layers, then pour the bouillon mixture over all. Cover and bake at 325° for 1½ hours. Stir twice during cooking time. Serve over hot rice, noodles or toast points.

Serves 5-6.

Ken Driscoll,
Athlete

Italian Oven Stew

Here is an ideal make-ahead meal in one dish for those after-the-game dinner parties. Serve with thick slices of French or dark whole grain bread and an assortment of fresh fruit.

3 large beef shanks
½ c flour
2 tbsp shortening
1 tsp salt
¼ tsp pepper
¼ tsp dry mustard
1 c water
4 bay leaves
3 lb zucchini, sliced
2 onions, sliced
1 (15½-oz) can garbanzo
   beans

1 (28-oz) can tomatoes
   and juice, chopped
¾ c butter or margarine
1½ c dry white wine
2¼ tsp salt
½ tsp pepper
3 cloves garlic, minced
1¼ tsp whole sweet basil
1 c grated Cheddar cheese
1 c grated Romano cheese
1½ c heavy cream

Flour both sides of the shanks and brown in the shortening. Lightly season each shank while browning with salt, pepper, and dry mustard. After they are well browned, add the water and 1 bay leaf. Cover, then bring to a boil and simmer for 1½ hours. Place the remaining ingredients, except the cheeses and cream, in a 4 qt baking dish, or divide equally into three 1½ qt dishes. Any unused portions may be frozen. Cover and bake at 400° for 1 hour, stirring once halfway through. Stir in the cheeses and cream and bake uncovered for 10 minutes longer. This stew may be prepared and cooked earlier and heated thoroughly before serving.

Serves 12.

Arvada McFarland,
Tyee

Lasagne

1 lb Italian sausage
1 (16-oz) can tomatoes, cut up
2 (6-oz) cans tomato paste
1 clove garlic, minced
1 tbsp dried basil leaves, crushed
2½ tsp salt
1 (10-oz) pkg lasagne noodles
2 eggs, beaten

3 c fresh ricotta or cream-style cottage cheese
½ c grated Parmesan or Romano cheese
2 tbsp dried parsley flakes
½ tsp pepper
1 lb mozzarella cheese, thinly sliced

For the meat sauce: Brown the meat slowly, then drain off any excess fat. Add the tomatoes, tomato paste, garlic, basil and 1½ tsp salt. Simmer, uncovered, for 30 minutes, stirring occasionally. Meanwhile, cook the noodles in boiling salted water until tender, then drain.

For the filling: Blend the eggs, 1 tsp salt and the remaining ingredients except the mozzarella.

To assemble: Layer ½ the noodles in a 9" x 13" baking dish. Spread with ½ the ricotta filling, ½ the mozzarella and ½ the meat sauce. Repeat. Bake at 375° for 30 minutes. Let stand 10 minutes before serving.

Serves 8-10.

Paul Skansi,
Athlete

Chili-Cheese Stack

Chili:
2 lb hamburger
½ c chopped green pepper
½ c chopped onion
2 tsp chili powder
1 tsp salt
4 (8-oz) cans tomato sauce
Dash of Tabasco sauce
2 (15-oz) cans kidney beans, drained
4 c grated Monterey Jack cheese

Crêpes:
4 eggs
1 c flour
1 c plus 2 tbsp milk
6 tbsp cooking oil

For the crêpes: Mix the eggs, flour, milk and oil with an electric mixer. Use a crêpe pan or pour 2 tbsp batter into a greased 6" skillet, tilting the pan to spread the batter. Cook the crêpes until done.

For the chili: Brown the meat and drain it. Add the green peppers and onions, cooking until they are tender. Add the chili powder, salt, tomato sauce, Tabasco and kidney beans. Bring the mixture to a boil, then simmer for 10 minutes. In an ungreased 8" x 13" pan, make 2 stacks, alternating between crêpe, then meat mixture, then cheese. End with cheese on the top crêpe. Don't skimp on cheese. More than 1 lb may be used. Heat the stack uncovered at 350° for 10–15 minutes. Cut the stack in wedges to serve. For easier serving, press each stack down so that it's no higher than 5"–6".

Serves 6–8.

Bonnie King,
Administrative Staff

Prairie Pizza

A fast and hearty whole wheat pizza from the Palouse. Personalize it with your choice of toppings. Our family prefers a vegetarian pizza with mushrooms, green and black olives, celery and green peppers.

2 c whole wheat flour
1 tsp salt
2 tsp baking powder
3 tbsp olive oil
¾ c milk
1 (12-oz) can tomato sauce
1 tsp Italian seasoning

1 tsp garlic salt
½ lb mozzarella cheese, grated
¼ lb sharp Cheddar cheese, grated
¼ c grated Parmesan cheese
Assorted toppings

Mix the whole wheat flour, salt, baking powder, olive oil and milk to form the crust. Press the mixture into a greased pizza pan. Spread the sauce evenly over the crust and sprinkle with Italian seasoning and garlic salt. Cover with grated mozzarella, then add grated Cheddar and Parmesan. Add the toppings of your choice. Bake in a 425° preheated oven for 18–20 minutes. Let the pizza cool for 10 minutes before slicing.

Serves 4.

Glenn Drosendahl,
News Media

Beef Stew

1 lb stewing beef
3 to 4 potatoes, diced
3 to 4 carrots, sliced
1 onion, chopped

1 small can peas, undrained
1 can tomato sauce
1 equal can water
Salt and pepper to taste

Combine all the ingredients in a baking dish and mix thoroughly. Cover and place in the oven. Bake at 225° for 5½ hours.

Serves 4.

Dee Stewart,
Tyee

Gloria Ehrig's Chicken Casserole

This was Gloria Vanderbilt's recipe but I changed it a little, so now it's mine.

3 c boned, cooked chicken
1 c carrots, cooked
12 small white onions, cooked
2 large potatoes, cooked and
  cubed
1 c peas, cooked
1 c mushrooms, sliced
4 c crushed potato chips

Sauce:
6 tbsp butter
6 tbsp flour
¼ tsp thyme
½ tsp salt
⅛ tsp pepper
2 c chicken stock
1 c light cream

Layer the chicken, carrots, onions, potatoes, peas and mushrooms in a buttered casserole dish. Pour the sauce over the chicken and vegetables and top with the potato chips. Bake at 400° for 25 minutes.

For the sauce: In a medium saucepan, slowly melt the butter. Remove from the heat, then add the flour, thyme, salt, and pepper, stirring until smooth. Add the stock and cream, a small amount at a time, stirring after each addition. Return the mixture to the heat and simmer for about 3 minutes, stirring constantly until thickened.

Serves 6.

Gloria Ehrig,
Tyee

Hot Chicken Casserole

1 c chicken, cooked and diced
¾ c mayonnaise
¼ c hot water
½ c almonds, sliced and
   toasted
1 can cream of chicken soup
1¾ c cooked rice
1 tbsp lemon juice

1 c chopped celery
2 tsp chopped onion
½ tsp salt
3 hard-cooked eggs, chopped
2 tbsp diced pimiento
½ c potato chips or rice
   krispies, crushed

Place the chicken in a large mixing bowl. Combine the mayonnaise and hot water, then add to the chicken. Mix in the almonds, soup, rice, lemon juice, celery, onion, salt, eggs, and pimiento. Place mixture in a buttered casserole and top with the potato chips. Bake at 375° for 30-40 minutes. Tuna, ham or turkey may be substituted for the chicken.

Serves 6.

Anna S. Lucas,
Tyee

Chinese Chicken Casserole

1 tbsp butter
¼ c chopped onion
1 c diced celery
1 c cream of mushroom soup
1 c chicken bouillon
1 tbsp soy sauce

Dash of Tabasco sauce
⅛ tsp pepper
2 c cooked, cubed chicken
   breast
1 c crisp chow mein noodles
⅓ c cashew nuts

Melt the butter in a skillet. Sauté the onion and celery until soft. Add the soup, bouillon, soy sauce, Tabasco, pepper and chicken. Cook, stirring often, for 5 minutes. Place the mixture in a casserole and top with the noodles and nuts. Bake at 350° for 35 minutes.

Serves 4-6.

Marie (Mrs. Armand)
Minorchio, Tyee

Zucchini Quiche

1 c Bisquick
½ c chopped onion
½ c grated cheese
2 tbsp parsley
½ tsp salt
½ tsp seasoning salt

½ tsp oregano
1 clove garlic, minced
½ c vegetable oil
4 eggs, beaten
3 c zucchini, coarsely shredded
and squeezed dry

In a large mixing bowl, combine the Bisquick, onion, cheese, parsley, salt, seasoning salt, and oregano. Add the garlic, oil, and eggs. Fold in the zucchini, then spread the mixture in a 9" x 9" pan. Bake at 350° for 25-30 minutes. Serve cut into squares. This quiche freezes excellently and the squares are easily warmed in a microwave.

Serves 6-8.

Beth and George Briggs,
Tyee

Dennis Weaver's Organic Vegetable Dish

½ c margarine
2 c cubed onions
2 c cubed celery
1 c sliced green pepper
1 large can mushroom slices
or 1½ c sliced fresh
mushrooms
4 c cooked brown rice

1½ c mixed raw nuts
(almonds, cashews, sunflower
seeds, sesame seeds)
Johnny's season salt to taste
2 t McKay's chicken seasoning
2 fresh tomatoes, cut into
wedges
1½ c cubed Cheddar cheese

Sauté the onions, celery, pepper, and mushrooms in the margarine very slightly so they are still crisp. Mix with the rice, nuts and seeds, salt and seasonings. Place the mixture in a 9" x 13" Pyrex dish, then place tomato wedges and cheese cubes on top. Bake at 350° for 20-25 minutes or until cheese melts.

Serves 8.

Renée (Mrs. Robert D.) Larrabee,
Board of Directors

Vegetable Pie

1 small eggplant (approx 1 lb)
1/4 c salad oil
1 onion, chopped
1 clove garlic, minced
3 large mushrooms, sliced
1 small zucchini, sliced
3/4 tsp dried basil
3/4 tsp dried oregano
1/2 tsp salt

1/8 tsp pepper
3 large tomatoes (approx
1 1/4-lb), peeled, seeded and
chopped
4 eggs
1/2 c grated Parmesan cheese,
divided
1/2 lb mozzarella cheese,
grated

Cut the eggplant into 1/2" cubes. In a large frying pan, heat the salad oil over medium-low heat. Add the eggplant, onion and garlic. Cook, stirring often, until the vegetables are just tender, about 10 minutes. Add the mushrooms, zucchini, basil, oregano, salt and pepper. Cook, stirring often, until the vegetables are soft, about 6–8 minutes. Add the tomatoes. Simmer rapidly until almost all the liquid has evaporated, about 15 minutes, then let cool. Lightly beat the eggs with 1/4 c Parmesan cheese. Stir into the vegetable mixture. Pour 1/2 this mixture into a buttered 9" pie plate or an 8" square baking dish. Top with 1/2 the mozzarella cheese, vegetable mixture, and then the remaining cheeses. Bake in a 400° oven (375° for a glass dish) for 25 minutes or until puffed and browned. Cool on a rack for 10 minutes before serving.

Serves 8.

Sally (Mrs. Philip) Lindquist,
Tyee

Easy Chicken and Spinach Crepes

Crepe Batter:
1 ¼ c flour
Pinch of salt
3 eggs, beaten
1 ½ c milk
2 tbsp butter, melted

Filling:
2 c diced cooked chicken
1 pkg frozen chopped spinach,
  cooked and drained
1 can cream of chicken soup
¼ c slivered almonds or water
  chestnuts
¼ c white wine
Dash of salt and white pepper
¼ tsp paprika
½ tsp Worcestershire sauce

For the crepes: Place all the ingredients in a blender or mixer and beat well. Let the batter stand for 1 hour. Use a crepe pan, or pour 2 tbsp batter into a 6" skillet, tilting to spread the batter. Cook the crepe on 1 side for 1 minute. Crepes may be frozen or refrigerated for later use.

For the filling: Mix all the ingredients together in a saucepan and heat. Spoon some filling into the center of the crepes, reserving some filling to spread on top. Roll crepes and place some filling on top.

Serves 4-6.

Brenda Barth,
Tyee

Chicken Artichoke Casserole

1 large and 1 small can
  artichoke hearts, quartered
3 chicken breasts, cooked and
  cut into pieces
½ c white wine
½ green pepper, chopped
1 small onion, chopped
1 tbsp butter
¾ c grated Cheddar cheese

White Sauce:
¼ c butter
¼ c flour
½ tsp salt
½ tsp pepper
1 ½ c milk
Wine, drained from chicken

Line a buttered 9" x 12" pan with artichoke hearts. Layer with the chicken, then pour wine over, cover with foil and refrigerate for at least 8 hours or overnight. Drain the wine from the chicken for the white sauce. Sauté the green pepper and onion in the butter for 2-3 minutes. Add to the white sauce, then pour it over the chicken and artichoke mixture. Sprinkle with the grated cheese and bake at 325° for 25 minutes, covered.

For the White Sauce: In a medium saucepan, slowly melt the butter. Remove from the heat and add the flour, salt, and pepper. Add the milk and reserved wine a small amount at a time, stirring after each addition. Return the mixture to the heat, and bring to a boil. Reduce the heat and simmer for 3 minutes, stirring constantly.

Serves 6.

Lynn (Mrs. James) Lambright,
Coaching Staff

Hood Canal Shrimp Casserole

½ c melted butter
4 to 5 oz Cheddar cheese
10 to 12 slices bread, torn
  into small pieces
1 (13-oz) can evaporated milk
½ c water
1 tsp salt
1 tsp dry mustard

1 (1-lb) pkg frozen cooked
  shrimp
3 hard-cooked eggs, chopped
1 tbsp sherry (optional)
¼ c corn flakes, crushed
1 tsp paprika

Melt the butter and cheese together on very low heat, stirring to keep from sticking. In a bowl, soak the bread in a mixture of the evaporated milk and water; add the salt and dry mustard. Add the butter/cheese mixture to bread mixture then add the shrimp, stirring gently. Add the eggs and sherry. Lightly grease a 2½ qt casserole. Place the mixture in the casserole and sprinkle with crushed corn flakes, then dust with paprika. Cover the casserole and refrigerate overnight. Bake at 300° for 1 hour.

Serves 4-5.

Helen (Mrs. Richard) Blakey,
Tyee

Seafood Lasagna

½ lb lasagna noodles
2 c cottage cheese
1 (8-oz) pkg cream cheese
 (room temperature)
1 c finely chopped onions
1 egg, beaten
2 tsp basil
1 tsp salt

¼ tsp pepper
1½ c cream of shrimp soup
1½ lb crab
½ lb shrimp
1 c grated Cheddar cheese
1 c grated mozzarella cheese
4 tomatoes, sliced
1 tsp sugar

Cook the noodles according to pkg directions. Blend the cottage cheese, cream cheese, onions, egg, basil, salt, and pepper. In a separate bowl, combine the cream of shrimp soup, crab, and shrimp. Butter a large Pyrex dish and layer it with ½ the noodles, ½ the cottage cheese mixture, and all the crab and shrimp mixture. Top with the remaining noodles and cottage cheese mixture. Bake at 350° for 15 minutes. Top with grated cheeses. Bake at 350° for 45minutes. Cover the top with the sliced tomatoes and sprinkle with the sugar. Return to the oven for 5 minutes.

Serves 8-10.

Jeanie (Mrs. Dick) Reiten,
Tyee

Shrimp Harpin

2 to 3 large fresh shrimp,
 deveined
1 tbsp lemon juice
3 tbsp salad oil
¾ c rice, cooked
2 tbsp butter
¼ c minced green pepper
¼ c minced onion

1 tsp salt
⅛ tsp pepper
⅛ tsp mace
Dash of cayenne
1 c condensed tomato soup
1 c cream
½ c sherry
½ c slivered almonds
Dash of paprika

Cook the shrimp in boiling water for 5 minutes, then drain. Place shrimp in a 2 qt casserole and sprinkle with the lemon juice and oil, then chill. Sauté the pepper and onion in butter for 5 minutes. Add the onion mixture, cooked rice, salt, pepper, mace, cayenne, soup, cream, sherry, and ¼ c almonds to the casserole. Sprinkle the top with the remaining almonds and paprika. Bake at 350° for 55 minutes or until bubbly.

Serves 4-6.

Julianna (Mrs. James) Collier, Tyee

Creamed Seafood Casserole

1 pkg MJB white and wild rice
½ lb fresh mushrooms, sliced
1 jar pimientos, drained
1 lb crab
½ lb shrimp
½ c bread crumbs or
½ c grated cheese

Sauce:
½ c butter
2 c milk
1 tbsp Worcestershire sauce
3 dashes Tabasco sauce
½ tsp salt
⅛ tsp pepper
½ c sherry
¼ c chopped green onions

Prepare the rice according to pkg directions and set aside. Sauté the mushrooms, then add the pimiento. Make the sauce as directed below and combine the sauce, mushrooms, rice, crab and shrimp. Place the mixture in a 2–3 qt buttered casserole and top with either the bread crumbs or the cheese. Bake at 250° for 40 minutes.

For the sauce: In a medium saucepan, slowly melt the butter, then remove the pan from the heat. Add the flour and stir until smooth. Return to the heat, adding the milk a small amount at a time, stirring after each addition. Add the Worcestershire, Tabasco, salt, pepper, sherry, and green onions. Simmer, stirring constantly, for about 3 minutes.

Serves 10-12.

Alexa P. Hemphill, Tyee

Baked Seafood Casserole

1 c uncooked rice
1 c grated sharp Cheddar
  cheese
¼ c butter
1 green pepper, chopped
¼ c chopped celery
1 can Aunt Penny's white sauce
1 small can mushrooms
1 can cream of mushroom soup

1 can tuna
1 can shrimp
1 can crab or salmon
1 c mayonnaise
1 tsp Worcestershire sauce
Dash of cayenne
1 can sliced water chestnuts
2 tbsp sherry
Buttered bread crumbs

Cook and seaon the rice. Line a buttered casserole dish with the rice and sprinkle with the grated cheese. In a skillet, melt the butter and sauté the green pepper, onion, and celery. In a separate bowl, mix the white sauce, mushrooms, soup, seafood, mayonnaise, Worcestershire sauce, cayenne, water chestnuts, and sherry. Pour over the rice and cheese. Top with the crumbs. Bake at 350° for 35-45 minutes.

Serves 6.

Pat (Mrs. Ralph) Oswald,
Administrative Staff

Hot Crab Souffle

8 slices bread
2 c crab or shrimp
½ c mayonnaise
1 onion, chopped
1 green pepper, chopped
1 c chopped celery

3 c milk
4 eggs
1 can cream of mushroom
  soup, undiluted
¾ to 1 c grated cheese
Dash of paprika

Dice ½ the bread into a baking dish. Mix the crab or shrimp, mayonnaise, onion, green pepper and celery together. Spread over the diced bread. Trim the crusts from the remaining bread and place the trimmed slices over the crab mixture, completely covering the surface. Mix the eggs and milk together and pour over the mixture in the baking dish, then refrigerate overnight. Bake in a 325° oven for 15 minutes, then remove from the oven and spoon 1 can mushroom soup and 1 can drained mushrooms over the top. Sprinkle grated cheese on top. Return the casserole to the oven for approximately 45 minutes or until the liquid is set.

Diced chicken may be substituted for the seafood. Add a dash of Worcestershire and sherry to the egg and milk if using chicken.

Serves 10-12.

Mrs. Charles P. Moriarty, Tyee

Crab Souffle

8 slices bread
3 c fresh crab
1 c finely diced celery
1 medium-size onion, chopped
1 medium-size green pepper chopped
½ c mayonnaise
Pimiento (optional)

4 eggs, well beaten
3 c milk
1 can cream of mushroom soup
1 small can mushrooms
1 lb Tillamook Cheddar cheese, grated

Cube 4 slices of bread and put them in the bottom of a 12" x 12" casserole. Mix together the crab, celery, onion, green pepper, mayonnaise, and pimiento. Spread the mixture over the bread in the casserole. Cube the remaining 4 slices of bread and place on top of the above. Beat the eggs, then add the milk and pour into the casserole. Refrigerate the casserole overnight. Remove from the refrigerator and let stand at room temperature for 30 minutes. Bake at 325° for 15 minutes, then remove from the oven and spoon 1 can mushroom soup and 1 can drained mushrooms over the top. Sprinkle grated cheese on top. Return the casserole to the oven for approximately 45 minutes or until the liquid is set.

Serves 8.

Clarice (Mrs. C. William) Campbell, Tyee

Crab and Tuna Casserole

¾ c cooked rice
2 tbsp onion flakes
1½ c sour cream
¾ c mayonnaise
1 tbsp lemon juice
Salt and pepper to taste
½ c sliced ripe olives

¼ tsp parsley
1 can sliced water chestnuts
½ lb mushrooms, sliced
1 (6½-oz) can tuna, drained
2 (6½-oz) cans crab, or
  ¾ lb fresh crab
½ c grated Cheddar cheese

Combine all the ingredients except the cheese. Bake covered at 350° for 1 hour. Five minutes before the casserole is done, sprinkle the grated cheese on top. Return the casserole to the oven uncovered. This dish may be prepared the day before and cooked the following day.

Serves 6.

Lana Schmid,
Member of the Cabinet

Shrimp and Crab Hotdish

1 c diced celery
1 green pepper, diced
1 large onion, diced
1½ lb or 2 cans mushrooms
2 garlic cloves, minced
2 tbsp butter
2 c cooked wild rice
2 c cooked white rice
2 c crab meat
2 c shrimp

1 can cream of mushroom
  soup
1 c blanched almonds
1 tsp curry
1 tsp Worcestershire sauce
¼ tsp parsley flakes
Salt and pepper to taste
½ c grated cheese
½ c buttered bread crumbs
4 tbsp sherry

Sauté the celery, green pepper, onions, mushrooms, and garlic in the butter. Add the rices, seafood, soup, almonds, curry, Worcestershire, parsley, salt, and pepper. Place in a buttered 9" x 13" baking dish. Sprinkle with grated cheese and buttered bread crumbs. Place the casserole in a pan of water. Bake at 350° for 40 minutes. Top with the sherry.

Serves 12.

Bea Gardner,
Tyee

ENTREES

Husky Barbeque

3 lb lean chuck, cut
   into ¾" cubes
1 tsp salt
1 c water
3 tbsp Worcestershire sauce

14 to 20 oz ketchup
2 tbsp vinegar
2 tbsp prepared mustard
Dash of Tabasco sauce
6 oz Coca Cola

Simmer the meat with the salt and water for about 2 hours, until very tender, adding more water if necessary. Shred the meat into a saucepan while still warm, being sure to remove all the fat and skin. Add the Worcestershire, ketchup, vinegar, mustard and Tabasco. Stir, then let simmer for 30 minutes. Add the Coca Cola. This is best prepared a day in advance, heated and served on buns with cheese.

Serves 6-8.

Val Kopp,
Tyee

Sweet and Pungent Spareribs

¼ c peanut oil
2 lb spareribs, cut in 1" pieces
¼ c chopped onion
¼ c chopped green pepper
1 c pineapple juice
½ c rice vinegar
¾ c water

2 tbsp ketchup
1 tbsp soy sauce
¼ tsp Worcestershire sauce
1 clove garlic, minced
½ c brown sugar, firmly
   packed
2 tbsp cornstarch

Heat the peanut oil in a skillet. Add the spareribs and brown well. Remove the spareribs and set aside, reserving 2 tsp drippings in the pan. Add the onion and green pepper and cook until tender. Add the pineapple juice, vinegar, water, ketchup, soy sauce, Worcestershire and garlic. Blend in the brown sugar and constarch. Bring the mixture to a boil, stirring constantly. Reduce the heat, then add the meat. Cook, uncovered, over low heat for 1 hour or until tender. Stir occasionally.

Serves 4-6.

Willie Rosoborough,
Athlete

Barbequed Spareribs

⅓ c vinegar
3 tbsp brown sugar
1 tbsp prepared mustard
½ tsp pepper
1 tsp garlic salt
¼ tsp cayenne pepper

1 lemon, sliced
1 medium-size onion, sliced
⅓ c butter
⅔ c ketchup
3 tbsp Worcestershire sauce
3–4 lb spareribs

In a medium-size saucepan, combine all the ingredients except the spareribs. Simmer for 15 minutes. Bake the spareribs on the rack of a broiler pan at 400° for 15 minutes. Place the ribs in a shallow baking pan and cover with the sauce. Marinate for several hours in the refrigerator. Bake at 325° for 30 to 60 minutes basting frequently.

Serves 6-8.

Derek Harvey,
Athlete

Polynesian Beef

1 (5-lb) brisket of beef
1 tsp garlic salt
⅛ tsp pepper
½ tsp paprika

1 pkg onion soup
3 tbsp soy sauce
3 tbsp brown sugar
2 c pineapple juice

Sprinkle the brisket with the garlic salt, pepper and paprika. Brown both sides under the broiler. Combine the onion soup, soy sauce, brown sugar and pineapple juice. Pour the mixture over the brisket. Bake at 325° for 2½ hours, or until tender. Cool the meat, and slice it into thin pieces. Reheat the meat in the drippings.

Serves 10-12.

Shirlee Bissell,
Administrative Staff

Scalloped Salmon

2 c coarsely-crushed salted
   cracker crumbs
⅓ c melted butter
1 tbsp minced parsley
1 tsp grated onion

Dash of pepper
1 (-lb) can salmon, drained,
   coarsely flaked
1 c light cream

Combine the cracker crumbs, butter, parsley, onion, and pepper.
Spread 1 c crumb mixture in a 9" pie pan or an 8" cake pan. Cover
with the salmon. Sprinkle the remaining crumbs on top, then pour
the cream over the crumbs.

Serves 6.

Joyce (Mrs. Eugene) Caruso,
Tyee

Petrale Sole Stuffed with Shrimp

1½ c celery
½ c chopped onion
3 c cooked shrimp
2 c water
1 c mayonnaise

1 c finely crushed potato chips
Pinch of cayenne pepper
16 small filets of sole
½ c butter, melted
1 tsp paprika

Boil the celery, onion and shrimp in the water for 1 minute. Drain,
then combine the shrimp mixture with the mayonnaise, chips and
pepper. Coat 8 individual ramekins with butter. Place a filet in each
ramekin, add stuffing, then cover with another filet. Pour butter over
the top of each filet and sprinkle with paprika. Bake at 350° for 20-25
minutes, being careful not to overcook.

Serves 8.

Merwyn Donley,
Tyee

Hawaiian Sweet-Sour Shrimp

2 tbsp salad oil
1 medium onion, sliced
1 green pepper, cut in 1" pieces
1 lb fresh green shrimp or
  prawns
3 tbsp rice vinegar
1 tbsp soy sauce
2 tbsp brown sugar

¼ tsp salt
1 clove garlic, crushed
⅛ tsp pepper
1 (13-oz) can pineapple,
  tidbits, undrained
2 tbsp cornstarch mixed with
  ¼ c cold water

In a wok or a skillet, sauté the onion and green pepper in the salad oil until tender, but not soft. Remove from the wok. Reheat the wok, then add the green shrimp and stir-fry until pink. Return the onion and green pepper to wok. Mix together the vinegar, soy sauce, brown sugar, salt, garlic, pepper, pineapple and cornstarch mixed with water. Add to the onions, pepper and shrimp in the wok and simmer, stirring until thickened.

Serves 6.

James Carter,
Athlete

Delicious Italian Shrimp

Simply delectable.

3 lb raw shrimp
¼ c oil (vegetable or olive)
4 cloves garlic, finely chopped

2 tsp oregano
2 tsp salt
¼ c chopped parsley

Peel the shells from the raw shrimp. Remove the vein from the back and pat the shrimp dry. In a saucepan, cook the oil, garlic, oregano and salt slowly for 8 minutes, stirring occasionally. Place the shrimp in a single layer in a shallow broiling pan. Pour the seasoned oil over the shrimp and mix well. Broil, stirring once or twice, until the shrimp have turned pink. Before serving, toss in the finely chopped parsley.

Serves 6.

Ray Horton,
Athlete

Lobster Thermidor

2 (1-lb) live lobsters
2 tbsp chopped onions
1 (3-oz) can mushrooms
2 tbsp butter
2 tbsp flour
¼ tsp salt
⅛ tsp pepper
⅛ tsp paprika

½ c light cream
½ c chicken broth
½ tsp Worcestershire sauce
1 egg yolk, beaten
2 tbsp sherry
3 tbsp dry bread crumbs
1 tbsp grated Parmesan
    cheese

Place the lobster in a large pot and cover with water. Boil for 5 minutes, reduce heat and simmer for 5 minutes more. Drain and let cool, then remove the meat carefully and reserve shells. Separate the meat into small pieces and set aside. Sauté the onion and mushrooms in the butter until the onion is tender. Add the flour, salt, pepper and paprika. Simmer until the mixture is bubbly. Remove from the heat, and stir in the cream, chicken broth and Worcestershire. Heat the mixture to boiling, stirring constantly. Boil and stir for 1 minute, then remove from the heat. Stir at least half the hot mixture into the egg yolk. Blend the egg mixture into the remaining hot mixture. Add the wine and lobster meat and heat thoroughly. Place the lobster shells in a 9" x 13" baking pan. Fill each with the lobster mixture. Mix bread crumbs and cheese and sprinkle over the shells. Bake at 450° for 5-8 minutes.

Serves 4.

Roger Tarver,
Athlete

Gingered Scallops

6 tbsp butter
1 ½ lb scallops, thinly sliced
2 tbsp fresh ginger, grated

¼ tsp salt
⅛ tsp pepper
2 tbsp parsley, finely chopped

Heat the butter in a skillet or wok until sizzling. Add the scallops and ginger and sauté briefly, just long enough to heat the scallops through but not long enough for them to become brown. Season with salt and pepper, sprinkle with parsley, and serve.

Serves 4.

Dean Browning,
Athlete

Baked Whole Salmon

The amount of each ingredient depends upon the size of the fish.

1 whole salmon
Mayonnaise
Salt
Pepper
Johnny's Seafood Seasoning

Lemon, thinly sliced
Onion, thinly sliced
Butter
Pale dry sherry

Rub the cavity of the salmon with a generous amount of mayonnaise. Sprinkle the cavity and the outside of the fish with salt, pepper and a liberal amount of seafood seasoning. Place the lemon and onion slices inside the cavity. Grease a large piece of heavy duty foil. Place the salmon on the foil on a bed of lemon slices. Place more lemon slices on top of the fish. Dot with butter, then drizzle a generous amount of sherry over the fish. Wrap the foil tightly around the fish and place it in a pan in case of leakage. Bake in a preheated 350° oven for 1 hour. This recipe may also be used on a hooded barbeque, leaving the foil open and basting the fish with a sauce of sherry, lemon juice and seasoned salt.

Lee Fields,
Tyee

Crab Stuffed Chicken

4 chicken breasts
  halved, skinned, and boned
½ c sliced green onions
¼ lb mushrooms, thinly sliced
¼ c butter
3 tbsp flour
¼ tsp thyme

½ c chicken broth
½ c milk
½ c dry white wine
Salt and pepper
1 can crab, drained
¼ c parsley
⅓ c bread crumbs
4 oz Swiss cheese, grated

Pound the chicken to ¼" thickness. Sauté the onion and mushrooms in the butter until all juices are evaporated. Stir in the flour and thyme, then add the broth, milk and wine. Cook, stirring until the mixture thickens. Season with salt and pepper. Stir together ½ c sauce, crab, parsley and bread crumbs. Spoon equally into the chicken pieces, then roll the chicken around the filling. Place rolls, seam side down in a greased 8" x 12" baking dish. Pour the remaining sauce over the chicken. Sprinkle with cheese, then cover. Bake at 400° for 40 minutes or until done.

Serves 4.

Linda West,
Tyee

Crab Foo Yung

6 eggs
¼ tsp Tabasco sauce
8 oz crab meat
1 c fresh bean sprouts

4 green onions and tops, thinly
  sliced on the bias
2 tbsp salad oil

Beat the eggs with the Tabasco, then stir in the crab, sprouts, and onions. Heat 2 tbsp oil in a small skillet, and add one quarter of the egg mixture. Cook until lightly browned, then turn and brown the other side. Remove to a hot platter.

Serves 4.

Tony Caldwell,
Athlete

Barbequed Crab

2 crabs
1 large onion
4 stalks celery
3 cloves garlic
4 tbsp oil
1 can consommé
2 small cans tomato sauce

1 tbsp whole red peppers
1 tbsp peppercorns
2 bay leaves
1 tbsp Worcestershire sauce
10 drops Tabasco sauce
3 tbsp soy sauce

Crack and clean the crab. Chop the onion, celery and garlic and sauté in the oil. When soft, add the consommé, tomato sauce, red peppers, peppercorns, bay leaves, Worcestershire and Tabasco. Bring to a slow boil, lower heat and simmer for 30 minutes. Add the soy sauce, then strain the liquid. Dump the cracked crab into a large pot. Pour the strained sauce over the top and let the crab do a back-stroke in a 300° oven for 45 minutes, glooping the sauce over all the pieces 3 or 4 times. Serve in bowls with lots of French bread.

Serves 4.

John Owen,
News Media

Clams with Black Bean Sauce

20 to 25 littleneck or
   cherrystone clams
3 tbsp vegetable or peanut oil
2 large cloves garlic, minced
1" ginger, peeled and minced

1 tbsp fermented black beans,
   minced
1 tbsp soy sauce
Dash of chili pepper powder
Chinese parsley

In a saucepan, cover the clams with boiling water and cook until the shells open. Remove the clams immediately and drain in a colander. Heat the oil in a skillet or wok. Add the garlic, ginger and black beans and stir rapidly. Add the soy sauce and chili pepper powder, then the clams and stir until they are thoroughly heated. Serve garnished with Chinese parsley.

Serves 2-4.

Richard W. Miller,
Tyee

Crisp Baked Chicken

3 to 3½ c grated day-old bread
¾ c grated Parmesan cheese
¼ c chopped parsley
1½ tsp salt

¼ tsp pepper
1 clove garlic, crushed
1 c butter, melted
2½ - 3 lb chicken pieces

Spread the crumbs in a flat pan and let dry for a few hours. Mix the crumbs with the cheese, parsley, salt and pepper. Add the crushed garlic to the melted butter. Dip the chicken pieces in the butter, then roll them in the crumb mixture. Place on a shallow, foil-lined baking pan. Refrigerate for 30 minutes. Pour the remaining butter over the chicken and bake in a 350° oven for 1 hour or until done. Do not turn the chicken, but baste it frequently with the pan drippings. Remove the pieces from the pan immediately and drain on wire racks. Serve hot or cold.

Serves 6.

Don Dow,
Athlete

Chicken Mole

1 (3 to 4-lb) roasting chicken,
   cut-up
2 tbsp peanut butter
1 tbsp sugar

1 can La Victoria Mole
   Poblano
1 small can tomato sauce
2-3 c chicken broth

Place the chicken in a 5-6 qt pot with enough water so it is immersed. Cover and bring the water to a boil. Reduce the heat and simmer for 45 minutes or until the chicken is tender. Remove the chicken and keep it warm, retaining the chicken broth. In a skillet on low heat, melt the peanut butter and sugar. Add the Mole Poblano, mixing thoroughly, and simmer. Add the tomato sauce and reserved chicken broth and let thicken; if needed, add more broth. Place the chicken pieces in the sauce and simmer. Serve with refried beans and Spanish rice.

Serves 6.

Tim Cowan,
Ahtlete

Sour Cream Chicken

8 chicken breasts
1 jar dried beef
8 slices bacon

1 can mushroom soup
1 pt sour cream

Bone and halve the chicken breasts. Line a shallow glass baking dish with a thin layer of dried beef. Wrap each chicken breast with ½ slice bacon and place it in the dish on top of the beef. Combine the soup and sour cream and pour over the chicken. Bake at 275° for 3 hours, covered for the first 1½ hours.

Serves 6-8.

Janet Shannon,
Coaching Staff

Windsor Canadian Goose
Absolutely delicious!

1 (6 to 8-lb) goose
1 qt buttermilk
1 (8-oz) pkg dried prunes
2 apples, sliced
5 slices bacon
2 tbsp butter

Sauce:
½ c butter
¼ c flour
¾ c chicken or beef broth
4 tbsp currant jelly
¼ tsp salt
1 c sour cream

Soak the goose in the buttermilk for at least 4 hours in the refrigerator. Wash and drain the bird. Stuff it with the prunes and apples. Truss and wrap it in the bacon. Cover it tightly with heavy foil and bake until tender at 325° for about 3 hours. Baste with butter during the last 30 minutes to brown. Remove the fruit from the goose. Arrange it around the bird on a platter, and serve the sauce immediately.

Sauce: Melt the butter in a saucepan. Stir in the flour with a whisk. Add the broth, then heat the mixture, stirring constantly. Just before serving, add the currant jelly, salt, and sour cream.

Serves 8.

Mary Lou (Mrs. Walter) Hinds
Tyee

Lemon Baked Chicken

This is good for diets, no fat or oil used.

1 chicken, cut up
Garlic salt
Paprika

½ tsp oregano
4 tbsp lemon juice
1 c water

Season the chicken pieces with the garlic salt, rubbing it well into the flesh. Sprinkle each with paprika, then place in a shallow baking pan, skin side down. Combine the oregano, lemon juice and water and pour over the chicken. Bake, uncovered, at 380° for 1 hour or longer, depending on the size of the chicken. Turn the chicken after 20 minutes.

Serves 4.

Ruth (Mrs. William)
Gerberding,
President's wife

Chicken Breasts Sauterne

Delicious served over steamed white rice.

3 chicken breasts, skinned
    and halved
½ tsp salt
Dash of pepper
Dash of paprika
½ c butter

2 cloves garlic, crushed
1 can cream of mushroom
    soup
1 can mushrooms with broth
1 c sour cream

Season the chicken breasts with the salt, pepper and paprika. Brown the pieces in the butter, then add the crushed garlic. Combine the soup, mushrooms, wine and sour cream in a large deep buttered casserole and add the browned chicken pieces. Cover and bake at 350° for 1 hour.

Serves 4-6.

Maryon Kopay,
Tyee

Mexican Chicken

Great with rice.

1 chicken, cut up and skinned
½ c flour
Salt and pepper to taste
Dash of paprika and thyme
4 strips bacon, cut in small
  pieces
3-4 carrots, cut into large
  pieces

2 tbsp chopped fresh parsley
1 bay leaf
1 small can peeled green chili
  peppers
1 lemon, thinly sliced
2 c tomato juice
  (approximately)

Dust the chicken with the flour mixed with the salt, pepper, paprika and thyme. Brown in a small amount of oil, then place in a dutch oven. Add the bacon, carrots, fresh parsley and bay leaf. Spread the green chili peppers over all. Sprinkle with the remaining flour and cover with lemon slices. Pour the tomato juice to almost cover the mixture. The flour will thicken it during cooking. Cover and bake at 350° for 1 hour, until tender.

Serves 4.

Myrtle W. Burke,
Tyee

Glazed Breast of Chicken with Grapes

4 large chicken breasts,
  boned and skinned
½ c flour
½ tsp salt
¼ tsp nutmeg

6 tbsp melted butter or
  margarine
2 tbsp orange marmalade
2 c seedless grapes,
  washed & drained

Cut the chicken meat lengthwise in strips about ½" wide. Dust with a mixture of flour, salt, and nutmeg; shake off any excess. In a large frying pan, lightly brown the strips in melted butter. Push the strips to one side and add the grapes; stir to heat through. Gently mix the grapes and chicken with the orange marmalade. Arrange the strips of chicken on a warmed serving platter with the grapes alongside.

Serves 4-6.

Dottie McLean,
Tyee

Ham Loaf in Raisin Sauce

1½ tbsp flour
1½ c brown sugar, packed
¾ tsp ground cloves
3 c seedless raisins
2½ c cornflake crumbs
6 eggs, beaten
3 c milk

⅓ c each minced onion
  and green pepper
3 lb fully cooked ham, ground
1½ lb lean pork, ground
1½ lb veal, ground
4 tsp salt
1 tsp pepper

Mix the flour, sugar, cloves and raisins and sprinkle the mixture evenly over the bottoms of 2 greased 9" x 13" baking pans. Mix remaining ingredients lightly, but thoroughly. Divide and press into the pans firmly. Bake at 325° for about 1½ hours. Let loaf stand a few minutes, then turn out of the pan and cut into 12 squares.

Serves 24.

Rena Lude,
Administrative Staff

Lamb Shish Kebab

1 leg of lamb
2 large onions
2 green peppers
16 large mushrooms
2-3 zucchini
Marinade:
½ c salad oil
¼ c lemon juice

1 tsp salt
1 tsp marjoram
1 tsp thyme
½ tsp pepper
1 clove garlic, minced
½ c chopped onion
¼ c snipped parsley

Have your butcher bone the leg of lamb. Cut it in 1½" cubes. Combine all the ingredients for the marinade, then add the meat, stirring well to coat the lamb. Refrigerate for at least 4 hours, turning the meat occasionally. Cut the vegetables into 1½" pieces and coat them with marinade. Fill skewers with meat cubes and broil over hot coals to medium rare, turning frequently and basting with marinade. Place the vegetables on separate skewers and broil on the cooler sides of the barbeque. By cooking the lamb and vegetables separately, the vegetables do not burn.

Serves 6-8.

Kit Green,
Administrative Staff

Marinated Pork

Juice of 6 oranges
Juice of 1 lime
Juice of ½ lemon
1 onion, sliced
1 bay leaf

½ tsp oregano
1 tsp salt
⅛ tsp pepper
1 (4-lb) loin of pork
2-3 cloves garlic, slivered

In a large ceramic or glass dish, combine all the juices. Add the onion, bay leaf, oregano, salt and pepper. Make small slits in the pork and insert the slivers of garlic. Place the pork in the juice mixture, turning it to coat. Chill the pork, covered with plastic wrap, for 12 to 14 hours, turning it occasionally. Drain the pork, reserving the marinade, and place it on a rack in a roasting pan. Roast the pork at 350° for 2½ hours, basting it every 15 minutes with the reserved marinade and skimming off the fat.

Serves 6-8.

Jim Rogers,
Athlete

Sauce for Barbequed Spareribs, Pork, Beef or Lamb

Allow about ½ lb ribs for each person unless you're feeding a hungry Husky. Then allow whatever's fair!

½ c soy sauce
⅓ c pineapple juice
2 tbsp sugar

1 clove garlic, crushed
3 lb spareribs

Mix all the ingredients together and stir thoroughly. Pour over the ribs. Marinate for 1 hour or longer. Barbeque or oven roast the ribs for 1 hour at 325°, basting occasionally.

Serves 5-6.

Roger Tarver,
Athlete

Teriyaki Tenderloin

½ c dry sherry
¼ c soy sauce
2 tbsp dry onion soup mix

2 tbsp brown sugar
2 lb tenderloin

Combine the sherry, soy sauce, soup mix, and brown sugar. Pour into a bag set in a deep bowl. Add the meat and marinate in the refrigerator for 8-24 hours. Place the meat on the rack of a roaster pan and bake at 425° for 50 minutes. Baste it occasionally with half the marinade. Add 2 tbsp water to the remaining marinade and bring it to a boil. Slice the meat and spoon the sauce over it.

Gail McHenry Walters,
Coaching Staff

Steak Spaghetti Sauce

1 lb round steak cut in
  small cubes
3 tbs olive oil
2 cloves garlic, minced
1 large onion, chopped
¼ lb mushrooms, sliced
1 (28-oz) can tomatoes,
  Progresso preferred
1 (8-oz) can tomato sauce
1 bouillon cube

½ c hot water
½ tsp salt
¼ tsp pepper
¼ tsp cayenne
¼ tsp allspice
2 tbsp chopped parsley
½ tsp sage
1 tsp thyme
¾ c sherry

In a large pot, brown the meat in the olive oil. Stir in the garlic and onion. Continue to cook and stir until the onion is lightly browned. Add the mushrooms, tomatoes, tomato sauce and the bouillon cube dissolved in the hot water. Add the salt, pepper, cayenne and allspice. Bring to boil, then lower heat and simmer, uncovered, for 2 hours. Add the parsley, thyme and sherry 15 minutes before serving over hot spaghetti.

Serves 6.

Tony Alvarado,
Athlete

Round Steak in Mirepoix

Mirepoix is a classic mixture of vegetables and liquid used in French cooking as a flavor enhancer. For a decorative appearance it is important that the vegetables be cut exactly as directed.

½ c carrots
½ c celery
½ c onion
3 tbsp butter or margarine
¼ bay leaf
2 c beef broth made with 2
    boullion cubes and 2 c water

2 lb round steak, cut ½" thick
Salt
Freshly ground pepper
Garlic powder
¼ c flour

Dice the carrots, celery and onion into tiny, even squares of less than ¼". Melt 1 tbsp butter in a saucepan and sauté the vegetables slowly until limp, then add the bay leaf and beef broth. Simmer the mirepoix for 5 minutes. Trim most excess fat from the sides of a round steak but leave a little for flavor. Slash the sides to prevent curling and leave the bone in to add flavor. Sprinkle the steak with salt, pepper and garlic powder. Dredge the seasoned steak in flour. Melt 2 tbsp butter in a medium-hot fry pan and brown the steak on both sides. Add the mirepoix, cover and simmer over low heat until tender, usually 1 to 1½ hours. Cut into large pieces and serve with some of the vegetables placed on top of each piece.

Serves 4-6.

Pat Wilson,
Administrative Staff

Barbeque Sauce on Beef Brisket

1 (4-lb) brisket of beef
1¼ c ketchup
¾ c corn syrup
¾ c chili sauce
¾ c wine vinegar
¾ c water, or more
½ c lemon juice

¼ c A-1 Sauce
1 tbsp celery seed
¼ c mustard
2 tbsp soy sauce
1 clove garlic, minced
Dash of Tabasco sauce

Wrap the brisket in foil and bake at 250° for 4 hours. Cool and slice into thin pieces. Arrange the slices in an ovenproof casserole dish. Combine the ketchup, syrup, chili sauce, vinegar, water, lemon juice, A-1 sauce, celery seed, mustard, soy sauce, garlic and Tabasco sauce. Pour the sauce over the meat. Heat thoroughly. Simmer in a 250-300° oven for 1-2 hours.

Serves 6.

Janet Shannon,
Coaching Staff

El Gaucho Recipe for Sparerib Barbeque Sauce

6 tbsp tomato paste
6 tbsp water
6 tbsp brown sugar
1 tbsp tarragon vinegar
3 tbsp chopped onions
1 tbsp Worcestershire sauce

1 tbsp soy sauce
1 tsp dry mustard
1 clove garlic, minced
¼ tsp salt
¼ tsp chili powder
Dash of Tabasco sauce

Mix all the ingredients together well. Good for oven baked ribs or as a baste for barbequed spareribs. For oven baking, cover ribs and bake at 350° until tender, about 1-2 hours.

Makes about 1 cup.

Brian Stone,
Athlete

Danish Meat Roll-Ups

This is an old, authentic Danish family recipe. It has been used many times for family dinners and parties. It is very easy to make and requires little work on the day of a party and actually improves with refrigeration or freezing. It has not been published before.

Roll-ups:
2 lbs beef round steak
1 medium-size onion
3 slices bacon
12 stems fresh parsley
¾ tsp salt
1 tsp pepper
2 tbsp flour
¼ c shortening or oil
String to tie roll-ups

Gravy:
2 tbsp flour
2 tbsp shortening or oil
1½ c hot water
¼ c sherry
1 (4-oz) can mushroom buttons
½ tsp salt
⅛ tsp pepper
1 (16-oz) can small new
    potatoes (optional)

For the roll-ups: Have the butcher cut the round steak into ¼" slices. Cut the slices into about 20-24 2½" pieces. Cut the onion into ¼" wedges, the bacon into ½" pieces, and remove the parsley from the main stem. Assemble the roll-ups as follows: Mix ½ tsp each of salt and pepper and lightly sprinkle the meat. Place 1 wedge of onion, 2 bacon pieces, and several pieces of parsley on each piece of meat, roll and tie with string. Mix the flour and remaining salt and pepper and lightly coat the roll-ups. Brown in the oil in a large frying pan or a dutch oven. Remove the roll-ups and use the same pan to make the gravy.

For the gravy: Add the shortening to the residue in the pan. Add the flour and brown the mixture. Add the water and cook until thickened. Stir in the sherry, mushrooms and juice, salt and pepper. Place the roll-ups in a covered casserole, pour the gravy over, and bake at 350° for 1 hour. Remove from the oven, cool and take off the strings. Return to the casserole. Add additional sherry or water if needed, and the potatoes. Return casserole to the oven and bake for 15 minutes, until heated thoroughly.

Serves 6-8.

Katie Whitworth,
Tyee

Flank Steak Marinade

1¼ c oil
½ c Worchestershire
2 tsp salt
½ c red wine vinegar
2 cloves garlic, crushed
¾ c soy sauce

2 tbsp Dijon mustard
2 tsp freshly ground pepper
2 tsp freshly chopped parsley
⅓ c fresh lemon juice
2 (1½ lb) whole flank steaks

Combine all the ingredients except the steak in a shallow glass dish. Add the steak and marinate in the refrigerator for 6-8 hours or overnight. Broil the steak 3" from the heat for about 5 minutes. Turn and broil about 5 minutes more. Carve in very thin slices.

Serves 5-6.

Rena Lude,
Administrative Staff

VEGETABLES

Artichokes Stuffed with Ricotta

6 large artichokes
4 tbsp wine vinegar
6 tbsp olive oil
1 clove garlic, peeled
1 bay leaf
5 whole peppercorns

½ lb Ricotta cheese
1 egg, slightly beaten
¼ c grated Parmesan cheese
¼ tsp salt
1-2 tbsp fresh bread crumbs
Butter

Remove the outer leaves and trim the tops, bottoms and leaf points of the artichokes. Place them in a pot filled with enough water to cover, then add the vinegar, oil, garlic, bay leaf, and peppercorns. Bring the liquid to a slight boil and cook the artichokes until tender, about 30 minutes. Cut the artichokes in half from top to bottom and remove the fuzzy choke with a spoon. Place the artichokes in a buttered baking dish with the cut side facing up. Mix the Ricotta cheese with a wooden spoon until soft. Then add the egg, Parmesan cheese and salt. Place a spoonful of the mixture on each artichoke half. Sprinkle bread crumbs over all and dot with butter. Bake at 350° for 20 minutes.

Serves 12.

Val Kopp,
Tyee

Green Bean Casserole

2 (16-oz) cans green beans,
  drained
1 (3½-oz) can whole
  mushrooms, drained
1 (8-oz) can water chestnuts,
  drained and diced

1 (10¾-oz) can cream of
  mushroom soup
½ c milk
1 tbsp soy sauce
1 can french fried onion rings

Mix together all ingredients except onion rings. Place in a buttered 2½ qt casserole and bake for 30 minutes at 325°. Top with onion rings during the last 10 minutes of baking.

Serves 8.

Darlene (Mrs. James R.)
Hermsen, Tyee

Tomato Pudding

Great with chicken or fish.

1 large can tomatoes	1 tsp salt
2 tbsp raisins	½ tsp ginger
2 tbsp brown sugar	3 c cubed bread
2 tbsp vinegar	½ c butter

Simmer the tomatoes, raisins, brown sugar, vinegar, salt, and ginger in a saucepan until the tomatoes cook down and the raisins are plump. Melt the butter and pour over the bread cubes, then add to the tomato mixture. Pour into a 1½ qt buttered casserole. Bake at 350° for 45 minutes.

Serves 10-12.

Phyllis Orrico,
Tyee

Fresh Broccoli with Cream Cheese Sauce

2 lb broccoli	2 tbsp lemon juice
4 tbsp butter	½ tsp monosodium glutamate
4 tbsp flour	or Accent
1 c cream	¼ c grated Parmesan cheese
1 bouillon cube	½ c grated Cheddar cheese
¾ c hot water	¼ c slivered almonds
2 tbsp dry sherry	

Separate and wash the broccoli. Cook it in a small amount of water until barely tender, about 4 minutes. Drain. Arrange the broccoli in a shallow baking dish and set aside. Melt the butter in a saucepan and blend in the flour. Pour in the cream and bouillon cube dissolved in the hot water. Cook until the mixture is smooth and thickened, stirring constantly. Add the sherry, lemon juice and monosodium glutamate. Pour the sauce over the broccoli. Sprinkle the grated cheeses and almonds over the top. If the dish is made ahead, refrigerate at this point. Bake at 350° for 20-30 minutes or until hot.

Serves 8.

Madelyn Handy,
Tyee

Broccoli Puff

Even broccoli haters like this one.

1 (20-oz) pkg broccoli florets
1 can cream of mushroom or
  cream of chicken soup
1½ c shredded grated sharp
  Cheddar cheese

½ c mayonnaise
2 eggs, beaten
2 tsp minced onion
Salt and pepper to taste

Cook the broccoli according to pkg directions. Drain. Combine all the ingredients and pour into a 9" x 13" baking dish. Bake 350° for 40-45 minutes or until a knife inserted in the center comes out clean.

Serves 10-12.

Michelle Reynolds,
Tyee

Broccoli Casserole

2 pkg frozen chopped broccoli
1 can cream of mushroom soup
½ c mayonnaise
1 tbsp lemon juice
½-1 c grated sharp
  Cheddar cheese

1 c Ritz cracker crumbs
  (approx 20)
¼ c slivered almonds

Cook the broccoli according to pkg directions. Drain. Arrange in a buttered casserole. Mix the soup, mayonnaise, lemon juice and cheese, then spoon the mixture over the broccoli and top with the buttered cracker crumbs and nuts. Bake at 350° for 20 minutes.

Serves 8.

Marla Lange,
Tyee

Cottage Cheese Broccoli Casserole

Great when served with fish or beef. Takes the place of rice, potatoes or noodles.

1 pkg frozen chopped broccoli
6 eggs
4 c small-curd creamed
  cottage cheese
6 tbsp flour

½ lb sharp Cheddar
  cheese, diced
½ c soft butter or margarine
2 green onions, chopped

Place the frozen broccoli in a strainer and pour boiling water over it to defrost. Drain, then place in a 9" x 13" buttered pan. Beat the eggs, then add the cottage cheese, Cheddar cheese, butter and onions. Pour the mixture over the broccoli and bake at 350° for 1 hour.

Serves 8-10.

Marian (Mrs. Chuck) Olson,
Tyee

Golden Crumb Broccoli

5 lb fresh broccoli, chopped
2 cans cream of mushroom soup
1 c mayonnaise
1 c grated Cheddar cheese

2 tbsp chopped pimiento
2½ tsp lemon juice
1 c Cheez-its crackers,
  crushed

Cover the broccoli with water in a saucepan and cook for 10-15 minutes or until tender. Drain and place the broccoli in a 9" x 13" pan. Combine the soup, mayonnaise, cheese, pimiento and lemon juice. Pour the mixture over the broccoli. Sprinkle the cracker crumbs over the top. Bake at 350° for 35 minutes, covered. This dish may be prepared a day ahead and baked when ready to serve.

Serves 12.

Lana Schmid,
Member of the Cabinet

Broccoli and Rice

1 small onion, chopped
1 c chopped celery
1 tbsp margarine
1 can cream of mushroom soup
½-1 tsp salt

1 pkg frozen chopped broccoli
1⅓ c Minute Rice
½ c sharp cheese, grated
¼ c slivered almonds

Cook the Minute Rice according to pkg directions. Cook, then drain the broccoli. Brown the onion and celery in the margarine. Add the soup, salt, broccoli and rice and mix well. Place in a greased casserole and sprinkle with cheese and almonds. Cover and bake at 350° for 1 hour.

Serves 6.

Rena Lude,
Administrative Staff

Casserole of Vegetables au Gratin

¼ c butter or margarine
¾ c green pepper, diced
¼ c flour
⅔ c milk
¾ tsp salt
⅛ tsp each pepper, basil
  and oregano

¼ tsp sugar
1 c grated Cheddar cheese
1 c solid pack canned
  tomatoes, drained
1 (9-oz) pkg frozen corn, thawed
2 (1-lb) cans whole onions,
  drained

Melt the butter or margarine in a pan. Add the green pepper and cook slightly, then stir in the flour. Add the milk, salt, pepper, basil, oregano, and sugar. Heat and stir until the sauce thickens. Remove from the heat and stir in ½ c cheese until melted. Add the tomatoes and heat the mixture again until thickened. Pour into an 8-c casserole. Add the corn and onions. Sprinkle the top with the remaining ½ c cheese. Bake, uncovered, in a 350° oven for 50 minutes.

Serves 6-8.

Joanne and Rick Harder,
Tyee

Deviled Corn

½ c margarine
2 tbsp flour
1½ c milk
1 tsp dry mustard

1 tbsp Worcestershire sauce
1 can cream-style corn
1 egg, beaten
½ c buttered bread crumbs

Melt the margarine in the top of a double boiler. Blend in the flour and cook for 5 minutes. Add the milk and cook for 10 minutes more, stirring constantly. Remove from the heat and cool. Add the mustard, Worcestershire sauce, corn and egg. Pour into a buttered baking dish and top with the crumbs. Place in the oven in a pan of water and bake at 325° for 30 minutes.

Serves 6.

Dora K. (Mrs. Elmer A.) Conner,
Tyee

Noodles with Cottage Cheese and Sour Cream

1 (8-oz) pkg medium noodles
2 c small curd cottage cheese
2 c sour cream
½ tsp salt
⅛ tsp pepper

¼ c melted butter
¼ c chopped onion
1 clove garlic, minced
1 tsp Worcestershire sauce
Dash of Tabasco sauce

Cook the noodles in boiling salted water for 10 minutes. Drain the noodles and rinse them in cold water. In a bowl combine all the other ingredients. Stir in the noodles and place the mixture in a buttered baking dish. Bake at 350° for 45 minutes. Serve hot with a side dish of grated Parmesan cheese.

Serve 8.

Anthony Allen,
Athlete

Tasty Rice Casserole

Good served with chicken or pork chops.

1 c chopped onion
¼ c butter
4 c cooked rice
2 c sour cream
1 c cottage cheese

1 (8-oz) can dried
  green chilies
Salt and pepper to taste
1½ c grated Cheddar cheese

Sauté the onions in the butter. Add the rice, sour cream, cottage cheese, chilies, salt, pepper, and 1 c Cheddar cheese. Place in a casserole and bake at 350° for 25 minutes. Add the remaining ½ c cheese and bake for 10-15 minutes more.

Serves 6-8.

Betty Ryan,
Member of the Cabinet

Stuffed Green Peppers with Rice

These are especially good as an accompaniment with lamb, ham or poultry.

3 large green peppers
2 c cooked rice
2 tbsp butter
1¼ c milk
½ c grated Cheddar cheese

½ tsp salt
Dash of pepper
¼ c minced onion
¼ c minced parsley
2 eggs, beaten

Cut the green peppers in half lengthwise and remove the seeds. Parboil until tender, but firm. Drain well and arrange in a greased baking dish. Blend the remaining ingredients well and spoon into the peppers. Bake at 300° for 30 minutes or until filling is firm.

Serves 6.

Elvi Olsson,
Tyee

Spanish Rice

1 lb bulk sausage
½ c diced onion
1 green pepper, diced
½ c diced celery
2½–3 c tomato juice
1 tbsp Worcestershire
  sauce

1 tbsp ketchup
1–2 tsp chili powder
1 c uncooked rice
1 sliced fresh or canned
  zucchini
½ c grated mozzarella
  cheese

Fry the sausage in a skillet. When browned, remove from skillet and set aside. In the same skillet add the onion, green pepper and celery and cook until the vegetables are tender. Pour the tomato juice over the vegetables. Add the Worcestershire sauce, ketchup and chili powder. Bring to a rolling boil, then add the rice and sausage. Cover and simmer for about 1 hour, until most of the liquid is evaporated. Add the zucchini and mozzarella and simmer 10 minutes more.

Serves 8.

Marti (Mrs. John A.) Sutton,
Tyee

Rice Romanoff

3 c cooked rice
¼ c finely chopped green onions
1½ c cottage cheese
1 clove garlic, crushed
1 c sour cream

¼ c milk
¼ tsp Tabasco sauce
½ tsp salt
½ c grated Parmesan cheese

Combine the rice and green onions. Blend the cottage cheese with the garlic, sour cream, milk, Tabasco and salt. Stir into the rice mixture. Place the mixture in a greased 1½ qt casserole. Sprinkle the top with Parmesan cheese. Bake at 350° for 25 minutes.

Serves 6.

Pat Moriarty,
Tyee

Rice, Cabbage and Cheese Casserole

2 c shredded cabbage
2 c whole canned tomatoes
1 tsp sugar
½ tsp salt
2 tbsp chopped onion

1 tbsp butter
1½ c cooked rice
¾ c grated sharp cheese
½ c dry bread crumbs
1 tbsp melted butter

Steam the cabbage in a small amount of water for 5 minutes and drain. Simmer the tomatoes with the sugar, salt, onion, and butter in a skillet for 5 minutes. Place the rice in a buttered casserole. Layer with ½ c cheese, cabbage, then the tomato mixture and top with bread crumbs combined with the melted butter and ¼ c cheese. Bake at 350° for 30 minutes.

Serves 6.

Mary (Mrs. Ralph B.) Potts,
Tyee

Rice with Pine Nuts

¼ c butter
2 tbsp minced onion
1 c uncooked rice
2½ c beef
  or chicken consommé

½ c toasted pine nuts
¼ c parsley, chopped
Salt and pepper to taste

In an ovenproof dish, melt the butter and sauté the onion for 1 minute. Add the rice and consommé, then cover the dish and bake in a preheated 350° oven for 45 minutes. Stir in the pine nuts and parsley and season with salt and pepper.

Serves 6.

Sharon P. Seaman,
Tyee

Wild Rice with Nuts and Herbs

¼ c wild rice
½ tsp salt
3 c chicken broth
1 medium-size onion,
  chopped
½ c minced celery

½ c broken walnuts
½ c slivered almonds
½ tsp rosemary
¼ tsp marjoram
1 tbsp chopped parsley
1½ tbsp butter

Soak the wild rice in water for 1½ hours. Drain, then place it in a saucepan with the salt and chicken broth. Bring mixture to a boil and simmer, covered, until tender. Drain and place the rice in a buttered casserole. Sauté the onions and celery in the butter until tender. Stir the nuts and herbs lightly into the rice. Add more salt, if desired. Cover and bake at 325° for 15 minutes. Before serving, stir the rice with a fork to release the steam. It should be fluffy.

Serves 6-8.

Nan B. Grayston,
Member of the Cabinet

Party Rice-Brashem

½ c butter
1 c uncooked rice
1 pkg Lipton Soup,
  onion or chicken

3 c water
¼ tsp curry

Melt the butter. Add the rice, soup, and water. Cook until evaporated, about 45 minutes. Add the curry and mix thoroughly.

Serves 6.

Franchon Kadish Rosen,
Tyee

Stuffed Shells

1 c finely chopped onion
3 tbsp olive oil
2 (6-oz) cans tomato paste
1 (1-lb 13-oz) can plum
  tomatoes
4 c water
1 tbsp sugar
2 tsp salt
⅛ tsp pepper
1 bay leaf
½ tsp oregano

¾ lb large pasta shells
  or rigatoni
5 qts boiling salted water
1 lb ricotta cheese
2 eggs, beaten
2 (10-oz) pkg frozen chopped
  spinach, cooked and
  drained
2 tbsp chopped parsley
¾ c grated Parmesan cheese

For the sauce: Sauté the onion in hot oil until soft. Add the tomato paste, tomatoes, water, sugar, 1 tsp salt, bay leaf, and oregano. Cover and simmer for 1 hour.

For the shells: Cook the shells in 5 qts boiling water for 10 minutes. Drain and rinse in cold water.

For the filling: Combine the ricotta cheese, eggs, spinach, parsley, ¼ c Parmesan cheese, 1 tsp salt and pepper. Stuff the shells with the cheese mixture. Layer the stuffed shells and sauce in a buttered 9" x 13" casserole. Sprinkle with the remaining ½ c Parmesan cheese. Bake 40 to 45 minutes.

Serves 6-8.

Mereda (Mrs. W.W.) Metz,
Tyee

Kidney Bean Casserole

6 slices bacon
6 green onions
2 (15-oz) cans kidney beans,
  drained

1 (15-oz) can whole kernel
  corn, drained

Dice the bacon and cut the green onions into ¼" slices. Fry the bacon and onions until the bacon is almost crisp. Drain off any excess fat. Place the kidney beans and corn in a buttered casserole. Add the bacon and green onions and mix lightly. Bake, uncovered, for 30 minutes at 350°.

Serves 6-8.

Marilyn (Mrs. Kenyon L.)
Anderson, Tyee

Stuffed Mushrooms

24 to 30 large mushrooms
1 large pkg cream cheese

1 pkg frozen chopped
  spinach, thawed
2 tbsp butter, melted

Wash the mushrooms and remove the stems. Press any excess moisture from the spinach. Mix the spinach and cream cheese together. Pour the melted butter into a 9" x 13" pan. Stuff the mushrooms with the spinach/cheese mixture and place them in the casserole. Bake at 350° for 12-15 minutes.

Serves 8-10.

Margaret (Mrs. Willis R.) McClarty, Tyee

Stir-Fried Black Mushrooms and Snow Peas

2 oz dried Chinese mushrooms
¾ c water
1 tbsp soy sauce
1 tsp sugar
1 tsp Accent
1 tsp sherry

1 tsp cornstarch
1½ tbsp oil
½ tsp salt
1 clove garlic, crushed
1 (10-oz) pkg frozen snow peas,
  thawed
½ can water chestnuts, sliced

Soak the mushrooms in warm water for 20 minutes and then drain and slice. In a small bowl, mix together ½ c water, soy sauce, sugar, Accent, sherry and cornstarch and set aside. Heat the oil, salt and garlic in a skillet. Add the mushrooms and stir-fry for 2 minutes. Add ¼ c water, cover and cook over low heat for 2 minutes. Add the soy sauce mixture and stir-fry until the gravy is clear. Add the peas and chestnuts and mix well, until just heated. Be careful not to over-cook the peas. Sliced jicama may be substituted for the water chestnuts.

Serves 6.

Beverly (Mrs. A. Pat) Miller Tyee

Spinach Casserole

¼ c butter
¼ lb American cheese
3 eggs
3 tbsp flour

1 pt small curd cottage cheese
1 pkg frozen chopped
  spinach, thawed
1 c bread crumbs

Cut the butter and cheese into coarse pieces. Add the eggs, flour and cottage cheese and mix well. Stir in the spinach and place the mixture in a greased casserole. Top with the bread crumbs browned in butter. Bake at 350° for 1 hour. This may be prepared ahead of time and refrigerated. If the recipe is doubled, bake for ½ hour longer.

Serves 6.

Marilyn (Mrs. Kenyon L.)
Anderson, Tyee

Spinach Artichoke Casserole

1 can artichoke hearts, drained
3 pkg frozen spinach, thawed
1 can cream of mushroom soup
Salt and pepper to taste

1 lemon, juiced
1 c sour cream
1 c mayonnaise
Dash of paprika

Line the bottom of a casserole with the artichoke hearts. Mix the drained spinach, soup, salt and pepper together. Pour the mixture over the artichokes. Combine the sour cream and mayonnaise with the lemon juice, then pour over with spinach. Sprinkle the top with paprika. Bake at 325° for 20 minutes.

Serves 12.

Catherine G. (Mrs. Harry E.)
Worley, Tyee

Baked Walla Walla Supreme

This is a good side dish which complements almost any meal.
It keeps well if you are not ready to serve it immediately.

4 c sliced Walla Walla sweet
  onions (approx 4–5)
3 tbsp butter (approx)
½ can cream of chicken soup
½ c milk

1 tsp Worcestershire sauce
¾ c grated Swiss cheese
4 slices french bread
Parmesan cheese
Dash of paprika

Sauté the onions in the butter until limp and tender. Place them in a buttered 8½" x 8½" casserole. Combine the soup, milk and Worcestershire. Pour the mixture over the onions. Top with grated cheese. Press the bread slices on top of the onion/cheese mixture. Lightly butter the top of each slice. Sprinkle with Parmesan cheese and paprika to taste. Bake in a preheated 350° oven for about 25 minutes, until the bread is browned.

Serves 8.

Jean (Mrs. Keith) Douglas,
Tyee

Scalloped Onions

3 tbsp and 2 tsp butter
3 tbsp flour
1 c chicken broth or consommé
¼ c dry sherry
¼ c grated Parmesan cheese

2 tbsp chopped parsley
Salt and pepper to taste
2 (1-lb) cans small whole
  onions, drained
¼ c dry bread crumbs

Melt 3 tbsp butter in a saucepan, then stir in the flour. Gradually add the broth and sherry. Cook, stirring constantly, until the mixture boils and thickens. Add the cheese, parsley, salt and pepper. Add the onions and mix well. Place the mixture in a greased casserole. Melt 2 tsp butter and mix with the bread crumbs, then sprinkle over the casserole. Bake at 350° for 25 minutes.

Serves 8.

Luellen Charneski,
Tyee

Cheese-Stuffed Baked Potatoes

Featured on the Santa Fe Railroad menu in the 1800s.

6 medium-size potatoes
(approx 2 lb)
1 (8-oz) pkg cream cheese,
softened or
1½ c low-fat cottage cheese

½ c butter, softened
1 tbsp chopped green onion
½ tsp salt
Dash of pepper
Paprika

Bake the potatoes at 400° for 45 minutes or until tender. Remove from the oven and knead them gently. Slash the top and carefully scoop the pulp from the potato shells. Reserve the shells. With a fork, mash the pulp. Blend in the cream or cottage cheese, butter, onion, salt and pepper. Omit the butter if using cottage cheese for a low-calorie recipe. Refill the potato shells and sprinkle with paprika. Reheat at 400° for 15-20 minutes.

Serves 6.

Dan Caldwell,
Athlete

Hashed Brown Potatoes

1 can cream of celery soup
⅓ c and 2 tbsp milk
1 (3-oz) pkg Philadelphia
cream cheese
Salt and pepper to taste

1 small onion, chopped
1 large pkg frozen hash brown
potatoes, separated but not
defrosted
¾ c grated Cheddar cheese

Mix the soup, milk, cream cheese, salt, pepper, and onion in a blender. Pour over the potatoes and mix in the Cheddar cheese. Refrigerate the mixture until ready to bake. Bake, covered, at 350° for 1 hour. Remove the cover if brownness is desired.

Serves 6-8.

Carol Linebarger,
Tyee

Potatoes Romanoff

4 medium-size potatoes
1 c sour cream
4 green onions, sliced
1 ¼ c grated sharp Cheddar
  cheese, divided

1 tsp salt
⅛ tsp pepper
Dash of paprika

Cook the potatoes in the jackets until tender, then peel and shred them. Combine the shredded potatoes with the sour cream, onions, ¾ c cheese, salt and pepper. Turn the mixture into a buttered 1½ qt casserole. Sprinkle with the remaining cheese and paprika. Bake, uncovered, at 350° for 30-40 minutes. This dish may be assembled ahead and refrigerated until time to bake and serve.

Serves 4-6.

Sharon Sproul,
Tyee

Potato Casserole

Delicious!

6 medium-size potatoes,
  cooked in skin, chilled, and
  grated after peeling
¼ c butter
2 c grated Cheddar cheese

2 c sour cream
⅓ c minced onion
1 tsp salt
¼ tsp white pepper

Combine the butter and cheese in a saucepan over low heat, and heat until almost melted. Remove from the heat and add the sour cream, minced onion, salt and pepper. Stir the mixture together, then pour it over the grated potatoes and blend thoroughly. Put the potato mixture in a buttered 9" x 12" casserole. Dot it with butter. Bake at 350° for 45 minutes. This dish may be prepared well ahead and baked at serving time.

Serves 6-8.

Gretchen Tapert Shaffer,
Tyee

Cheese Potato Crisp

1 lb potatoes	1 egg, lightly beaten
1 c milk	2 tbsp butter, melted
1 c grated Gruyere cheese	1 tsp salt
1 small onion, minced	¼ tsp pepper

Peel and grate the potatoes. In a bowl, combine the potatoes, milk, cheese, onion, egg, butter, salt, and pepper. Place the mixture in a buttered 1½ qt. baking dish and bake, covered with foil, in a pre-heated 350° oven for 1 hour. Remove the foil and bake the mixture for 30 minutes more, or until the top is golden.

Serves 4.

Rick Mallory,
Athlete

Crispy Potato Squares

¼ c vegetable oil	2 eggs, separated
6 medium-size potatoes, pared and shredded	2 tbsp flour
1 large onion, chopped	1 tbsp salt
	¼ tsp pepper

Pour 3 tbsp oil into an 8" x 8" pan and heat in a 425° oven while pre-paring the potatoes. Drain the potatoes and onions thoroughly, patting them dry with paper towels. Mix the potatoes and onions with the egg yolks, flour, salt, and pepper. Beat the egg whites until stiff but moist peaks form, then fold gently into the potato mixture. Remove the pan from the oven and spoon in the potatoes, then sprinkle the remaining tbsp oil over the top. Bake at 425° for 45-60 minutes or until tender and crispy-brown. Cut into squares and serve immediately.

Serves 6.

Barbara Farron,
Tyee

Sesame Potato Slices

6 medium-size baking
  potatoes
½ c butter, melted
3 tbsp finely chopped onion

3 tbsp chopped parsley
2 tbsp sesame seeds, toasted
1 tsp salt
1 c grated Cheddar cheese

Scrub and dry the potatoes. Slice each potato crosswise ½" thick. Place the slices on a piece of heavy duty foil. Combine the melted butter, onion, parsley, sesame seeds, and salt. Dip the slices of potato, one at a time, in the mixture to coat. Arrange the dipped potato slices on the foil so that the slices are staggered and a portion of each slice is exposed. Draw the foil up and fold several times to enclose the potato slices. Place on a baking pan. Bake in a preheated 325° oven for 30 minutes. Remove the pan from the oven and carefully unfold the foil to expose the slices. Return to the oven and continue baking for 1 hour or until the potato slices are tender. Sprinkle with the grated cheese during the last 15 minutes of baking time.

Serves 6.

Babs Fisher,
Tyee

Zucchini Casserole

4 c thinly sliced zucchini
2 eggs
1 c mayonnaise
1 c grated Parmesan cheese
Salt and pepper to taste

1 onion, chopped
¼ c chopped green pepper
1 tbsp butter
2 tbsp bread crumbs

Butter a 2 qt casserole. Spread the zucchini evenly in the casserole. In a blender or food processor, thoroughly blend together the eggs, mayonnaise, Parmesan cheese, salt and pepper. Add the onions and chopped green pepper. Pour the mixture over the zucchini. Dot with butter and sprinkle crumbs over the top. Bake at 350° for 30 minutes.

Serves 6.

Rosemary (Mrs. Patrick T.)
Easter, Tyee

Zucchini Casserole

2 c finely chopped zucchini
½ c Parmesan cheese
½ c Bisquick

1 egg, beaten
¼ c oil
Garlic powder (optional)

Mix together all the ingredients. Place in a 1½ qt greased casserole. Bake at 325° for 35 minutes.

Serves 4.

June (Mrs. V.W.) Markov, Tyee

Zucchini Soufflé

¼ c butter or margarine
¼ c unsifted all-purpose flour
1⅓ milk
1 tsp salt
Dash of pepper
1 tbsp grated onion

1¼ c grated zucchini,
  squeezed dry
5 eggs, separated
  (room temperature)
1 tsp cream of tartar
½ c grated sharp Cheddar
  cheese

Melt the butter in a medium saucepan. Remove from the heat and blend in the flour. Stir in the milk slowly, then cook over low heat, stirring until thickened. Add the salt, pepper and onion and stir until blended. Cool. Add the zucchini to the cooled mixture. Beat the egg whites at high speed with the cream of tartar until stiff peaks form. In a separate bowl, beat the yolks until thick and light. Blend into the zucchini sauce, then fold the mixture into the egg whites. Turn into a greased 1½ qt soufflé dish or casserole and top with the grated cheese. Set the dish in a pan containing 1" hot water. Bake at 350° for 1 hour.

Serves 6.

Jean (Robert G.) Reid, Tyee

DESSERTS & SWEETS

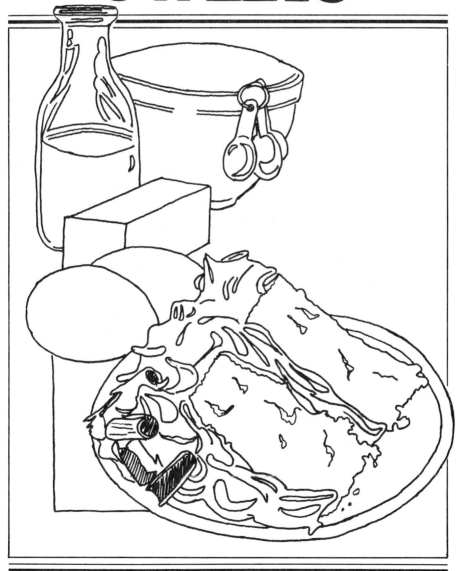

Pots de Crème

2 c light cream
2 (4-oz) bars sweet
chocolate, grated

Pinch of salt
6 egg yolks
1 tbsp Jamaican rum

Combine the cream, chocolate and salt in a heavy saucepan. Place over low heat and cook, stirring constantly, until thoroughly mixed and just about to boil, but do not boil the mixture. Beat the egg yolks slightly with a electric mixer. Add the chocolate, beating constantly. Cool, then stir in the rum. Pour the mixture into pots de crème or a large bowl. Refrigerate until firm.

Serves 6–8.

Mark Jerue,
Athlete

Burnt Crème

1 pt whipping cream
4 egg yolks

½ c sugar
1 tsp vanilla

Heat the cream over low heat until bubbles form around the edge of the pan. Beat the egg yolks and sugar together until the mixture is thick and yellow, about 3 minutes. Beating constantly, pour the cream into the egg yolks; add the vanilla and pour into 4 custard cups. Place the cups in a baking pan with ½–1" boiling water. Bake at 350° for 45 minutes. Remove the cups from the water and refrigerate. Sprinkle sugar on top of the crème and brown to a golden color under the broiler before serving.

Serves 4.

Gae Burr,
Administrative Staff

Lynn's Deluxe Cheesecake

As featured in Gourmet *magazine.*

Crust:
½ c butter
1¾ c graham cracker crumbs
½ tsp cinnamon
¼ c finely chopped walnuts

Filling:
3 large eggs
2 (8-oz) pkg cream cheese,
  room temperature
1 c sugar
¼ tsp salt
2 tsp vanilla
¼ tsp almond extract
3 c sour cream

For the crust: Melt the butter in a saucepan. Add the graham cracker crumbs, chopped walnuts and cinnamon. Reserve ¼ of the crust mixture for topping. Press the remaining mixture around the sides and bottom of a spring-form pan.

For the filling: Beat the eggs, cream cheese, sugar, salt, vanilla and almond extract together. This mixture must be absolutely smooth. Fold in the sour cream with a whisk, being careful not to break down the texture. Pour the filling into the crust, then finish with the remaining crust mixture. Bake at 375° for about 1 hour. The cake will either crack across the middle or around the edge. Cool, then chill 4–5 hours before serving.

Serves 16.

Lynn (Mrs. Robert J.) Lucurell,
Tyee

Damn Good Cheesecake

Crust:
¾ c all-purpose flour
3 tbsp sugar
½ tsp grated lemon peel
6 tbsp butter
1 egg yolk, lightly beaten
¼ tsp vanilla

Filling:
3 (8-oz) pkg cream cheese,
  room temperature
¼ tsp vanilla
¼ tsp grated lemon peel
1 c sugar
2 tbsp flour
¼ tsp salt
2 eggs plus 1 egg yolk
¼ c milk

For the crust: Combine the flour, sugar and lemon peel. Cut in the butter until the mixture is crumbly. Add the egg yolk and vanilla; mix well. Pat half the dough onto an 8" spring-form pan bottom. Bake at 400° for 7 minutes, or until golden brown. Butter the side piece to the pan and attach to bottom. Pat remaining dough into sides to a height of 1¾".

For the filling: Beat the softened cream cheese until smooth, then add the vanilla and lemon peel. Mix the sugar, flour and salt together and gradually blend into the cheese mixture. Add the eggs and yolk. Beat just until blended. Gently stir in the milk. Pour into the crust-lined pan. Bake at 450° for 10 minutes. Reduce heat to 300° and bake for 55 minutes more or until center appears set. Remove from oven and cool for 15 minutes. Loosen the sides of the cheesecake from the pan with a spatula. Cool for ½ hour more. Remove the side piece from the pan. Cool for 2 hours longer. Cover with Strawberry Glaze (recipe follows).

Serves 12.

Eric Michael Moran,
Athlete

Strawberry Glaze

for Damn Good Cheesecake

3 c strawberries	4 tsp cornstarch
½ c water	A few drops of red
⅓ c sugar	food coloring (optional)

Cut 2¼ c strawberries in half. Place the halved strawberries on top of the cooled cheesecake. Make the glaze by crushing the remaining ¾ c strawberries in a saucepan. Add the water and cook 2 minutes, then sieve. In a separate saucepan, combine the sugar and cornstarch. Gradually stir in the berry mixture. Bring to a boil, stirring constantly. Cook until thick and clear. Add food coloring if desired. Cool to room temperature. Pour glaze over strawberries on cheesecake. Chill for 2 hours or more.

Eric Michael Moran,
Athlete

Chocolate Mousse Marnier

6 squares semisweet chocolate	¼ c Grand Marnier
¼ c water	⅛ tsp salt
4 eggs, separated	3½ tbsp soft butter
¾ c plus 1 tbsp sugar	1 c whipped cream

Melt the chocolate with the water in a double boiler over hot, but not boiling, water. Mix the egg yolks in a small saucepan with ¾ c sugar. Heat gently, stirring until sauce thickens. Do not boil! Remove from heat immediately. Add Grand Marnier and salt. Beat butter into chocolate mixture. When smooth, add egg yolk mixture. Fold in the whipped cream. Beat the egg whites until frothy. Add the remaining sugar and beat until stiff but not dry. Fold into chocolate mixture. Spoon into individual mousse or custard cups. Chill.

Serves 6–8.

James P. Shaffer,
Tyee

Apricot Cheesecake

1½ c apricot nectar
¼ c plus 2 tbsp sugar
1 pkg Knox unflavored gelatin
1 tbsp lemon juice
2 tsp grated lemon rind

2 (8-oz) pkg cream cheese
2 egg whites
1 c whipping cream
1 c graham cracker crumbs

Mix the apricot nectar, ¼ c sugar, gelatin, lemon juice and lemon rind in a pan and bring to a boil, stirring constantly. Cook until the mixture thickens and is reduced by about ⅔. Set aside and allow to cool to lukewarm. Beat the softened cream cheese in a large bowl. Add the apricot mixture slowly and continue beating until well blended. Beat the egg whites and 1 tbsp sugar until stiff but not dry. Whip the cream with 1 tbsp sugar. Fold the egg whites, then the whipped cream, into the cheese/apricot mixture. Reserve 2 tbsp graham cracker crumbs; press the remainder into the bottom and sides of a 9" pie pan. Spoon filling into pan and sprinkle reserved crumbs over. Refrigerate for at least 4 hours.

This cheesecake may also be topped with any fruit: apricot halves, blueberries, strawberries, etc., plus your favorite glaze.

Serves 16.

Ramona Bachofner,
Tyee

Cherries Jubilee

1½ tsp grated orange peel
½ c orange juice
½ c sugar
1 (1-lb 14-oz) can pitted Bing
  cherries, drained

½ tsp cornstarch
1 tbsp water
3 tbsp brandy or Cognac
1 qt vanilla ice cream

In a medium saucepan, combine the orange peel, orange juice and sugar. Cook, stirring, over low heat until the sugar has dissolved. Add the cherries and simmer, uncovered, for 5 minutes. Remove from heat and drain, reserving liquid. In a small bowl, combine the cornstarch and water until smooth. Stir the cornstarch mixture into the reserved liquid from the saucepan and bring to a boil, stirring constantly. Reduce heat and simmer for 1 minute. Add the cherries and heat gently. Pour the cherry mixture into a chafing dish or bowl. Heat the liquor slightly over low heat, then pour over the cherries and ignite. Serve, flaming, over vanilla ice cream.

Serves 6.

Irma (Mrs. Dick) Erickson,
Coaching Staff

Husky Chocolate Pound Cake

3 c flour
3 c sugar
1 c cocoa
1 tbsp baking powder
1 tsp salt

1 c butter, room temperature
1½ c milk
1 tbsp vanilla
3 eggs
¼ c light cream

Sift together the flour, sugar, cocoa, baking powder and salt into a mixing bowl. Make a well in the center and add the butter, milk and vanilla. Beat the mixture for 5 minutes. Add the eggs, one at a time, and the cream, beating the mixture thoroughly after each addition. Pour the batter into a well-oiled 10" tube pan and bake at 325° for 1½ hours or until cake tests done. Cool completely on a wire rack before removing from pan.

Serves 6–8.

Sterling Hinds,
Athlete

No Crust Coconut Cream Pie

Coconut lovers will flip at the taste!

4 eggs
½ c flour
2 c milk
6 tbsp butter

½ c sugar
1 c coconut
1 tsp vanilla
1 tsp cinnamon

Place all the ingredients in a blender and blend for 3 minutes. Grease and flour a 10" pie plate, then pour in the mixture. Sprinkle with cinnamon. Bake at 350° for 40 minutes, let cool, and refrigerate for at least 1 hour. Serve plain or with whipped cream.

Serves 8.

Kathleen Dearborn,
Tyee

Rhubarb Custard Pie

2 tbsp flour
1 c sugar
½ tsp salt
¼ tsp nutmeg

2 eggs, beaten
3 c rhubarb, thinly sliced
1 (8") unbaked pie shell

Mix the flour, sugar, salt and nutmeg. Blend into the beaten eggs. Mix in the rhubarb. Spread the mixture in the pie shell. Bake at 450° for 15 minutes, then reduce heat to 350° and bake for about 30 minutes longer.

Serves 8.

John Gardenshire,
Athlete

Avocado Pie

2 large avocados
2 (8-oz) pkg cream cheese
¼ c honey, or
   1 c sugar

3–4 drops Tabasco sauce
1 tsp lemon juice
Graham cracker crust

Cream all ingredients except crust in a mixer or blender. Pour into crust and chill overnight.

Serves 8.

Melissa Sue Anderson,
Tyee

Frozen Strawberry Pie

1 c flour
2 tsp sugar
½ c butter
1 (3-oz) pkg cream cheese,
   room temperature

2 pkg frozen strawberries, unsweetened, semi-thawed
½ c sugar
2½ tbsp cornstarch
1 c whipping cream

Combine the flour and sugar. Add the butter with a pastry blender. Pat the mixture into a 9" pie plate and bake at 300° for 15 minutes. While the crust is still hot, spread the cream cheese over the bottom. Set pie aside to cool. Place the berries in a medium-size saucepan. Add the sugar and cornstarch. Stir over medium heat until the mixture boils. Remove from heat and stir occasionally while the strawberries cool. Pour into the pie shell and refrigerate until well chilled, at least 1 hour. Serve with whipped cream.

Serves 6–8.

Norlonna Klein,
Tyee

Peanut Butter Ice Cream Pie

1 qt vanilla ice cream,
  slightly softened
½ c chunky peanut butter
½ c crushed unsalted peanuts

1½ tsp vanilla
1 (10") graham cracker crust
Whipped cream
Maraschino cherries

Combine the ice cream, peanut butter, ¼ c peanuts and vanilla in a large bowl and mix well. Pour into the crust, sprinkle with remaining peanuts and freeze. Decorate with whipped cream and Maraschino cherries.

Serves 6–8.

Mark Stewart,
Athlete

Angel Pie

Meringue shell:
3 egg whites
1 c sugar
1 tsp lemon juice

Custard filling:
4 egg yolks
½ c sugar
4 tbsp lemon juice
2 tbsp grated lemon rind

1 c whipping cream

For the meringue shell: Beat the egg whites until stiff but not dry. Gradually beat in ½ c sugar. Add the remaining sugar alternately with the lemon juice. Continue to beat the mixture until stiff and glossy. Spread in a brown-paper-lined 9" round layer pan or greased pie plate. Bake in a 275° oven for 60 minutes. Cool.

For the custard filling: Beat the egg yolks until thick and lemon colored. Gradually beat in the sugar. Blend in the lemon juice and rind. Cook in a double boiler, stirring constantly, until thick—about 5–8 minutes. Cool. Beat the whipping cream until stiff. Spread ½ the cream over the meringue shell. Spread with the cooled lemon custard filling. Top with the remaining whipped cream. Chill for about 12 hours before serving.

Serves 8.

Gordon and Joan Culp,
Tyee

Sky-High Coconut Cream Pie

This is the famous pie from the Willows,
a noted Honolulu restaurant.

Pie:
3 c milk, scalded
½ c sugar
1 tbsp butter
Pinch of salt
1½ c grated fresh coconut
5 tbsp cornstarch
4 egg yolks
¼ tsp vanilla

1 (9") pie shell, baked and
cooled

Meringue:
6 egg whites
½ tsp salt
1½ tsp cream of tartar
¼ c sugar
½ tsp vanilla

Combine the milk, butter, sugar, salt and 1 c grated coconut in a saucepan. Let the mixture come to a near boil, stirring occasionally. Mix the cornstarch with a little water, add to the hot milk and continue cooking until thickened. Beat the egg yolks, then add a small amount of the hot mixture to the eggs, mixing well. Add the remaining hot mixture, then the vanilla. Cool the mixture for about 3 minutes more. Cool, then fill the pie shell. Top with the meringue and bake at 350° for about 10 minutes, or until the meringue is brown. Cool or chill before serving.

For the meringue: Beat the egg whites, salt and cream of tartar together until soft peaks form. Gradually add the sugar until the meringue is smooth and stands firm. Stir in the vanilla and remaining ½ c coconut.

Serves 8.

Aaron Williams,
Athlete

Cranberry Refrigerator Dessert

2 c fresh cranberries (approx
  ½ lb)
1 c diced bananas
1½ c sugar
2 c vanilla wafer crumbs

¾ c plus 2 tbsp butter or
  margarine
2 eggs
½ c chopped nuts
1 c whipping cream

Grind the cranberries. Combine with the diced banana and ½ c sugar; set the mixture aside. Combine vanilla wafer crumbs and 6 tbsp butter or margarine, melted. Press ½ the crumb mixture into the bottom of a 9" x 9" pan. Cream the remaining ½ c butter or margarine and the remaining 1 c sugar until light. Add the eggs and beat until fluffy. Fold in the chopped nuts. Spread over the crumb layer. Top with the cranberry mixture. Whip the cream until soft peaks form. Spread over all. Sprinkle with the remaining crumbs and press down slightly. Chill for 6 hours or overnight.

Serves 12.

Judy Johnson,
Tyee

Cranberry Chiffon Pie

Crust:
1½ c pecans, finely ground
5 tbsp sugar
1 tbsp butter, melted

Filling:
¾ c sugar
6 tbsp all-purpose flour
½ tsp salt
1½ c cranberry juice cocktail
½ c heavy cream, whipped
3 egg whites

For the crust: Combine the pecans, sugar and butter. Spread along the bottom and sides of a 9" pie plate. Bake at 350° for 10 minutes.

For the filling: Mix together ½ c sugar, flour and salt. Add the cranberry juice cocktail. Bring the mixture to a boil over medium heat, then cook until thickened and bubbly, stirring often. Cool, then add the whipped cream. Beat the egg whites until stiff. Add ¼ c sugar and continue beating until peaks are stiff and glossy. Fold into the cranberry mixture. Pour into the pie shell and chill. Serve with whipped cream if desired.

Serves 6–8.

Danny Greene,
Athlete

Chocolate Cream Pie

Crust:
1 c flour
¼ c finely chopped walnuts
1 sq unsweetened chocolate,
　coarsely grated
2 tbsp sugar
⅛ tsp salt
⅓ c shortening
2 tbsp cold water

Filling:
1¼ c sugar
⅓ c cornstarch

¼ tsp salt
3 c milk
3 sq unsweetened chocolate
4 egg yolks, slightly beaten
1 tbsp vanilla

Meringue:
4 egg whites, room
　temperature
¼ tsp cream of tartar
Dash of salt
½ c sugar
½ tsp vanilla

For the crust: In a bowl, mix the flour, walnuts, chocolate, sugar and salt. Cut in the shortening until the mixture resembles coarse crumbs. Sprinkle with the water, about 1 tbsp at a time, stirring until the mixture forms into a ball. On a lightly floured surface, roll the pastry into a large circle. Fit into a 9" pie plate and trim the edges. Prick the bottom and sides with a fork, then bake at 375° for 20–25 minutes or until lightly browned. Cool and set aside.

For the filling: In a heavy saucepan, mix the sugar, cornstarch and salt. Gradually stir in the milk until smooth. Add the chocolate and stir over medium heat until the mixture thickens and boils. Gradually blend some of the chocolate mixture with the egg yolks, then add to the remaining chocolate mixture. Stir over low heat for 2–3 minutes. Remove from heat and stir in the vanilla. Pour the filling into the pie shell.

For the meringue: In a small mixing bowl, beat the egg whites, cream of tartar and salt until foamy. Add the sugar, 1 tbsp at a time, beating until the mixture is stiff and glossy. Beat in the vanilla. Immediately heap the meringue onto the filling in the shell, spreading it carefully to the edges. Bake at 425° for 3–5 minutes, or until the meringue is lightly browned. Cool, then chill for at least 2 hours. Garnish the pie with chocolate shavings or crumbs of crust mixture.

Serves 6–8.

Don Vaughn,
Athlete

German Sweet Chocolate Pie

4 oz Baker's German sweet
  chocolate
⅓ c milk
1 (3-oz) pkg cream cheese,
  softened

2 tbsp sugar (optional)
1 (8-oz) container Cool Whip
1 graham cracker crust

Melt the chocolate with 2 tbsp milk in a double boiler over low heat, stirring often. Beat in the softened cream cheese and the remaining milk. Fold in the Cool Whip and spoon the mixture into the crust. Freeze for 4 hours. If the sugar is used, beat it into the cream cheese before adding cheese to chocolate mixture.

Serves 6–8.

Madeleine (Mrs. Vincent A.) Mennella, Tyee

Chocolate Frango Pie

1 c butter or margarine
2 c powdered sugar
4 oz unsweetened chocolate,
  melted and cooled

4 eggs, well beaten
1 tsp vanilla
1½ tsp peppermint extract
1 graham cracker crust

Soften the butter and beat in the powdered sugar. Add the cooled, melted chocolate. Add ¼ of the eggs at a time to the chocolate mixture, then add the vanilla and peppermint. Pour the mixture into the graham cracker crust. Chill.

Serves 8.

Anne Henderson, Tyee

Chocolate Mud Pie

1 (8½-oz) pkg chocolate
  wafers
½ c plus 3 tbsp butter or
  margarine
1½ pt coffee ice cream,
  softened

⅓ c cocoa
⅔ c plus 2 tbsp sugar
1⅓ c heavy cream
2 tsp vanilla extract
2 sq semisweet chocolate

In a covered blender or a food processor with a knife blade attached, blend the chocolate wafers to fine crumbs. Melt ½ c butter or margarine. In a 9" pie plate, mix the chocolate wafer crumbs and melted butter or margarine with a fork. Using hands, press the mixture into the bottom and sides of the pie plate. Bake at 350° for 10 minutes. Cool the crust completely on a wire rack. Carefully spread the ice cream into the crust; freeze until firm, about 1½ hours. In a 2-qt saucepan over medium heat, cook the cocoa, ⅔ c sugar, ⅓ c heavy cream and the remaining 3 tbsp butter or margarine until the mixture is smooth and boils. Remove from heat; stir in 1 tsp vanilla. Cool mixture slightly, then pour over ice cream. Return the pie to the freezer; freeze until firm, at least 1 hour. Just before serving, beat the remaining cream with 2 tbsp sugar and 1 tsp vanilla until soft peaks form. Spread the whipped cream over the pie and garnish with chocolate curls.

Serves 10.

Gordon and Joan Culp,
Tyee

Mud Pie

20 Oreo cookies
⅓ c plus 2 tbsp butter
½ gallon vanilla ice cream,
   softened

1½ tsp instant coffee
3 sq semisweet chocolate
1 c sugar
1 large can evaporated milk

Crush the cookies and mix with ⅓ c melted butter. Press into the bottom and sides of a 9" pie plate. Freeze. Thoroughly mix the ice cream and instant coffee. Pour over the Oreo crust and freeze again. Combine the chocolate, sugar, 2 tbsp butter and evaporated milk in a saucepan. Cook over medium heat until thick, quite a long time. Cool completely, then spread over the top of the ice cream. Freeze. Top with Dream Whip or whipped cream and/or nuts.

Serves 6–8.

Karen Murray,
Athlete

Peach Pudding

8 peaches, peeled and sliced,
   or 1 (1-lb 4-oz) can peach
   slices, drained, or 2 pkg
   frozen peach slices, thawed
   and drained

¼ tsp cinnamon
½ c sifted flour
½ c sugar
Pinch of salt
¼ c butter or margarine

Place the peaches in the bottom of a greased 1-qt casserole and sprinkle with the cinnamon. Sift the flour, sugar and salt into a mixing bowl. Cut in the butter or margarine until the mixture is mealy. Spoon the mixture smoothly over the peaches and, with a paring knife, poke 4 air holes in the surface. Bake at 450° for 15 minutes, then reduce the temperature to 375° and continue baking for 20–25 minutes, or until the top is crisp.

Serves 4.

Jan Fulton,
Athlete

Peanut Butter Pudding

⅓ c sugar
1½ tbsp cornstarch
¼ tsp salt

2 c milk
⅓ c peanut butter
1 tsp vanilla

Combine the sugar, cornstarch and salt in a saucepan. Gradually add the milk and cook over medium heat, stirring constantly, until thickened. Cook and stir for 2 minutes longer, then add the peanut butter and the vanilla. Pour the pudding into dessert dishes, cover and chill.

Serves 4.

Charles Clapp,
Athlete

Steamed Cranberry Pudding

Use this recipe at Christmas instead of plum pudding. It has a much milder flavor and is a family favorite.

Pudding:
½ c Waconia sorghum or
   light molasses
2 tsp soda
½ c hot water
1⅓ c bread flour
1 tsp baking powder
2 c chopped cranberries

Sauce:
1 c sugar
½ c butter
1 c cream

For the pudding: Mix all ingredients together quickly and steam in a tightly-covered mold for 1½ hours. Serve with the butter sauce.

For the sauce: Cook all the ingredients together in a double boiler over low heat for 15 minutes.

Virginia Hall,
Coaching Staff

Lemon Bars

Filling:
Zest of 1 lemon, grated
1 c sugar
2 eggs
3 tbsp lemon juice
2 tbsp flour
½ tsp baking powder

Crust:
1 c flour
½ c butter
¼ c powdered sugar

2 tsp powdered sugar, for
   topping

For the crust: Combine the flour, butter and powdered sugar in a food processor or a mixer. Pat the dough into a buttered 9" square pan. Bake at 350° for 15 minutes.

For the filling: Mix the grated zest and the sugar in the food processor or mixer. Add the eggs, lemon juice, flour and baking powder and mix thoroughly. Pour the filling over the crust and bake at 325° for 25 minutes. Cool and sprinkle the top with powdered sugar. Cut into bars.

Flossie (Mrs. Don) Smith,
Administrative Staff

Pumpkin Pie Tarts

*A delightful change from the usual pumpkin pie
at Thanksgiving time!*

1 pkg Dream Whip
1 pkg vanilla instant pudding
   mix
1 c canned pumpkin
⅔ c milk

½ tsp nutmeg
½ tsp ginger
½ tsp cinnamon
8–10 individual tart shells
Whipped cream for topping

Prepare the Dream Whip according to pkg directions. In a large mixing bowl, combine the pudding mix, pumpkin, milk and spices. Fold in 1 c Dream Whip. Spoon into the tart shells and chill for several hours or overnight. Serve with a dollop of whipped cream or remaining Dream Whip.

Serves 8–10.

Flossie (Mrs. Don) Smith,
Administrative Staff

Mocha Torte

Torte:
5 eggs
1 c sugar
1 tbsp instant coffee powder
½ c flour, sifted
½ c finely ground hazelnuts

Mocha Cream:
½ pt heavy cream
2 tbsp powdered sugar
½ tbsp instant coffee powder,
   dissolved in ½ tbsp rum or
   brandy

For the torte: Separate the eggs, then beat the whites until they form soft peaks. Gradually add the sugar, continuing to beat until the mixture is stiff. Beat the egg yolks until light and thick and fold into egg whites. Mix together the instant coffee powder, flour and nuts; thoroughly and gently fold into egg mixture until completely blended and no streaks remain. Pour gently into a greased and floured 9" tube pan with a removable bottom. Stir through the mixture to release any air bubbles. Bake in a preheated 325° oven for 50–55 minutes. Cool on a cake rack, then split into 4 layers and fill with mocha cream. Sift the powdered sugar over the top.

For the mocha cream: Beat the cream until thick, then slowly add the sugar, mixing thoroughly. Add the coffee powder dissolved in liquor and stir until smooth.

Makes 4 c.

Carole Taylor,
Tyee

Sacher Torte

Cake:
¾ c butter
¾ c sugar
6 eggs, separated
1 tsp vanilla
6 oz semisweet chocolate,
  melted and slightly cooled
1 c ground almonds
1 c flour
Apricot or raspberry jam

Frosting:
6 oz semisweet chocolate
¾ c heavy cream
½ c sugar
2 tbsp corn syrup
3 tbsp butter

For the cake: Cream the butter and sugar. Add the egg yolks one at a time, then the vanilla. Beat the egg whites until stiff and fold into the chocolate. Combine the two mixtures and add the almonds, mixing well. Pour into 2 buttered and floured 9" layer cake pans. Bake at 300° for 25 minutes. Remove cakes from the pans when cooled and spread with jam. Put the layers together and frost. Refrigerate frosted cake for 2–3 hours before serving.

For the frosting: Combine the chocolate, cream, sugar and corn syrup in a heavy saucepan and stir over heat until chocolate is melted. Remove from heat and add the butter. Allow to cool before frosting cake.

Nan B. Grayston,
Member of the Cabinet

Sacher Torte

Torte:
6 egg whites
¾ c sugar
½ c butter
1 c chocolate chips, melted
⅞ c flour, sifted

½ c apricot jam

Frosting:
1½ c chocolate chips
½ c strong coffee
2 tbsp butter

For the torte: Beat the egg whites until almost stiff. Gradually add the sugar and continue to beat until the meringue is thick and glossy. In another bowl, cream the butter. Add the melted chocolate and beat until fluffy. Gradually add the flour, beating very slowly until flour is incorporated, then at high speed for 1 minute. On low speed, add the meringue, beating only until blended into chocolate mixture. Pour into a well-buttered and floured 8" spring-form pan. Bake in an oven preheated to 400° but lowered to 325°when the cake is put in, for 50 minutes, or until a toothpick inserted in the center comes out clean.

For the frosting: In a double boiler, heat the chocolate chips, coffee and butter until melted. Remove from the heat and beat mixture until smooth and of spreading consistency.

Bill Stapleton,
Athlete

Girdle Stretcher Pie

8 Cinnamon Crisp graham
  crackers
½ c brown sugar
¼ c butter, melted

1 qt coffee ice cream,
  softened
1 jar chocolate fudge topping

Crush 7 crackers, then add the brown sugar and melted butter. Press the mixture into the sides and bottom of a 9" pie plate. Spread the ice cream in the pie shell and freeze. Warm the topping, then slowly pour it over the ice cream. Sprinkle with the remaining crushed cracker. Freeze. The pie may also be made in a square or an oblong pan.

Serves 6–8.

Carol (Mrs. Don) James,
Coaching Staff

Hawaiian Banana Cake

½ c shortening
1½ c sugar
1 tsp vanilla
2 eggs
2 c cake flour, sifted
1 tsp baking powder
1 tsp baking soda

½ tsp salt
½ c sour cream
1 c mashed bananas
  (approx. 5)
2 c whipped cream
3 bananas

Cream the shortening, sugar and vanilla until light and fluffy. Add the eggs and beat well. Sift the flour, baking powder, baking soda and salt together. Add the dry ingredients to the creamed mixture, alternating the additions with sour cream and bananas. Pour into 2 greased 8" layer pans. Bake at 350° for 30 minutes. Frost with sweetened whipped cream and sliced bananas.

Serves 8.

Leroy Lutu,
Athlete

White Fruit Cake

½ c butter
1 c sugar
1¾ c flour
1 tsp baking powder
½ tsp salt
½ tsp almond extract
½ tsp vanilla extract

½ c chopped almonds
¾ c coconut
½ c white raisins
½ c chopped candied cherries
½ c candied pineapple
5 egg whites, stiffly beaten

Cream the butter and sugar. Sift the dry ingredients and add to the butter and sugar. Add the almond and vanilla extracts. Stir in the almonds, coconut, raisins, cherries and pineapple. Fold in the stiffly beaten egg whites. Pour into a buttered and floured tube pan. Place pan in a pan of cold water. Bake for 5 hours in a 200° oven. If the oven is too warm, the white raisins will turn brown.

Dora K. (Mrs. Elmer A.) Conner,
Tyee

Prune Cake

1½ c sugar
3 eggs, beaten
1 tsp baking soda
1 c buttermilk
1 c corn oil
1 tsp cinnamon
1 tsp cloves

1 tsp allspice
1 tsp nutmeg
1 c mashed, cooked prunes
1 c chopped pecans
1 c flour
1 tsp baking powder

Add the sugar to the eggs and beat well. Slowly add the oil. Dissolve the baking soda in the buttermilk, then stir into the egg mixture with the spices, prunes, pecans, flour and baking powder. Pour the batter into a greased 9" ring pan. Bake at 350° for 40–45 minutes. Cool, then spread with icing.

Tom Riley, Athlete

Ladyfinger Lemon Cake

A delicious fluffy lemon cake

1 pkg ladyfingers
1 can sweetened condensed
  milk
4 eggs, separated

1 tsp freshly grated lemon
  rind
Juice of 3 large lemons
½ tsp cream of tartar

Lightly butter the sides of a 7" spring-form pan. Line the sides with the ladyfingers. Blend the condensed milk, egg yolks, lemon rind and lemon juice thoroughly. Beat the egg whites and fold in the cream of tartar. Gently fold the lemon mixture into the beaten egg whites. Pour the batter into the lined pan and bake at 375° for 20–30 minutes, until top is nicely browned. Chill in refrigerator or freezer.

Serves 8.

Gloria Ehrig,
Tyee

Crunchy Crusted Apple-Nut Cake

1 c butter
2 c sugar
3 eggs
3 c sifted flour
¾ tsp salt
1½ tsp baking soda

1 tsp cinnamon
¼ tsp nutmeg or mace
2 tsp vanilla
3 c chopped apples
2 c chopped walnuts

Cream the butter and sugar together until fluffy. Gradually beat in the eggs. Sift the flour, salt, baking soda, cinnamon and nutmeg or mace together. Gradually add the flour mixture to the creamed mixture. Stir in the vanilla, apples and nuts. The batter will be stiff. Bake in a greased, floured 10" tube pan at 325° for 1 hour 15 minutes. Let cool in the pan on a rack for 10 minutes. Remove from the pan; place the cake right side up on rack to complete cooling.

Serves 6–8.

Andy Bresolin,
Athlete

Carrot Pineapple Cake

Cake:
1½ c salad oil
2 c sugar
3 eggs
2 c drained, crushed
   pineapple
2 c grated carrots
2½ c flour
1 tsp baking soda
1 tsp salt

2 tbsp cinnamon
1 tsp vanilla
1 c chopped nuts

Frosting:
1 (3-oz) pkg cream cheese,
   softened
½ c butter
1 (1-lb) box powdered sugar
1 tsp vanilla

For the cake: Cream the oil, sugar and eggs thoroughly. Add the pineapple and carrots. Sift together the flour, soda, salt and cinnamon and add to the creamed mixture. Add the vanilla, beat well and add the nuts. Bake in a greased and floured 9"x13" pan or a bundt pan at 350° for approximately 45 minutes or until a toothpick inserted in the center comes out clean. A bundt pan will take about 55 minutes.

For the frosting: Cream together the cheese and butter. Add the sugar and vanilla and beat until smooth and creamy.

Serves 6–8.

Ray Cattage,
Athlete

Baked Fudge Dessert

2 c sugar
½ c flour
½ c cocoa
4 eggs, well beaten

½ lb butter, melted
2 tsp vanilla
1 c chopped pecans

Mix the sugar, flour and cocoa together. Add to the beaten eggs and blend thoroughly. Add the butter, vanilla and nuts. Pour mixture into a 9"x9" pan or glass baking dish and place dish in a pan of hot water. Bake in preheated 300° oven for 45 minutes or longer. The baked mixture should be of a custard consistency, but not quite as stiff. As it cools, it will become more firm. This dessert may be made a day ahead.

Serves 10.

Dr. William S. Church,
Tyee

Chocolate Layer Dessert

1 c flour
2 tbsp sugar
½ c margarine, melted
1 c chopped nuts
1 (8-oz) pkg cream cheese, softened
1 c powdered sugar

2 tbsp milk
1 (12-oz) carton Cool Whip
1 small pkg chocolate instant pudding
1 small pkg vanilla instant pudding
3 c milk

Mix together the flour, sugar, margarine and nuts. Spread this crumb mixture in a 9"x13" pan. Bake at 350° for 15–18 minutes. Set aside to cool.

Thoroughly mix together the cream cheese, sugar and 2 tbsp milk. Fold in ½ the Cool Whip and spread over the crumb mixture. Mix the chocolte pudding, vanilla pudding and remaining milk together, then pour over the cream cheese layer. Refrigerate until firm. Spread the rest of the Cool Whip over the top and sprinkle with nuts or chocolate shavings. Refrigerate overnight or freeze.

Serves 8–10.

Gail McHenry Walters,
Coaching Staff

Caramel Dumplings

Dumplings:
1 tbsp butter
½ c sweet milk
2 tsp baking powder
½ c white sugar
1¼ c flour
½ c nuts and coconut

Syrup:
1 c brown sugar
1 tbsp butter
2½ c hot water
½ c white sugar
1 tsp vanilla

Mix all dumpling ingredients together thoroughly and set aside. Mix all syrup ingredients together in a saucepan and boil for 5 minutes. Pour syrup into a 9"x13" pan and drop dumpling dough by spoonfuls into the syrup. Bake at 375° for 20 minutes or until slightly brown.

Makes 18.

Elizabeth Chicane,
Athlete

Danish Puff

2 c flour
1 c butter
1 c plus 2 tbsp water

1 tsp almond flavoring
3 eggs

Cut ½ c butter into 1 c flour. Sprinkle with 2 tbsp water and mix with a fork. Form dough into a ball and divide it in half. Pat the dough into 2 strips 12"x 3"and place them on an ungreased cookie sheet. Mix the remaining butter and water in a saucepan and bring to a boil. Add the almond flavoring and remove pan from heat. Stir in the remaining flour all at once. When smooth, add the eggs one at a time, beating well until smooth. Divide the mixture in half and spread over each dough strip. Bake at 350° for approximately 60 minutes or until top is brown. Top with powdered sugar icing and sprinkle with nuts.

Serves 8.

LaVonne (Mrs. Andrew V.) Smith,
Tyee

Coconut Macaroon Torte

4 egg whites
Pinch of salt
½ c sugar
3 tbsp light rum
1½ c sweetened shredded
   coconut
¼ c blanched almonds,
   ground

2 tbsp all-purpose flour
½ tsp lemon rind, grated
Fresh berries or sweet
   cherries
1 c whipped cream

Beat the egg whites with the salt in a large bowl until soft peaks form. Gradually add the sugar and beat until the peaks are stiff and shiny. Beat in the rum. Combine the coconut, almonds, flour and lemon rind, then fold gently into the egg white mixture. Butter and flour a 9" round cake pan. Spread the mixture evenly over the bottom. Bake at 350° for about 20 minutes until top is light brown. Cool torte in the pan on a wire rack. Unmold and mound with sweetened berries and whipped cream.

Serves 6.

Tom Burnham,
Athlete

Delight Dessert

¾ lb marshmallows
⅔ c orange juice
⅔ c ginger ale

½ c whipped cream
½ an angel food cake

Melt the marshmallows in the orange juice over low heat, then remove from heat and allow to cool. Add the ginger ale and fold in the whipped cream. Break the angel food cake into 1" chinks into the bottom of a Pyrex dish. Pour mixture over the cake and refrigerate for at least 2 hours or until firm. Serve with whipped cream and red cherries for color. This dessert may be made the day before.

Serves 15.

Jeanne (Mrs. Donald G.) Brown,
Tyee

Fancy Party Dessert

1 c milk
1 c sugar
2 pkg Knox gelatin
½ c cold water
1 pt whipped cream
1 c almonds, slivered
1 c coconut

Sauce:
1¼ c brown sugar
⅔ c light Karo syrup
4 tbsp butter
⅜ c heavy cream
⅜ c half-and-half

Heat the milk and sugar together. Pour over the gelatin, softened in the cold water. Mix well and place in the refrigerator. When gelatin is set, fold in the whipped cream. Add the almonds and coconut. Pour into 1 large mold or 12 small ones for individual servings. Refrigerate until firm.

For the sauce: Cook the brown sugar, Karo syrup and butter to the soft ball stage (230°–240°). Add the cream and half-and-half and stir until well blended. Pour the warm sauce over individual servings.

Serves 12.

Bea Gardner,
Tyee

Lemon Dessert

1 c flour
¼ c sugar
1 c coconut
½ c butter

1 large pkg lemon pudding
mix
1 pkg Dream Whip

Mix the flour, sugar and coconut together. Cut in the butter with a pastry blender until the mixture is in chunks the size of small peas. Spread over the bottom of a pie pan. Bake in a 350° oven for 10 minutes. Stir the mixture and return to oven for an additional 10 minutes to brown evenly. Set aside ½ the crust mixture. Make the pudding according to pkg directions. Reserve 1 c pudding. Pour remainder over the crumbs in the pie plate. Prepare Dream Whip according to pkg directions. Mix with the reserved pudding. Spread on top of the pudding and top with the remaining crumbs.

Serves 8.

Sharon Sproul,
Tyee

Blintz Loaf

Batter:
1 c butter or margarine
1 c sugar
4 eggs
1½ c milk
2½ c flour
2 tsp baking powder
1 tsp salt

Filling:
2 lb dry cottage cheese
4 tbsp butter
2 eggs
2 tbsp sugar
Pinch of salt

For the filling: Combine all the ingredients and mix well. Set aside.

For the batter: Sift the dry ingredients together. Cream the butter and sugar well. Add the eggs, then small amounts of the flour mixture and milk, alternately. Pour batter to cover the bottom of a 9"x13" pan, then some filling. Alternate layers until both are gone. Bake in a 350° preheated oven for 1 hour or until set. Cut loaf into squares and serve with sour cream and jam.

Serves 16.

Rose (Mrs. William V.) Sherman, Tyee

Baklava

1 lb walnut and/or almond
  meats, finely chopped
5 tbsp sugar
1 tsp cinnamon
Dash of ground cloves
1 lb phyllo pastry sheets

1½ c sweet butter, melted
Syrup:
  4 c sugar
  2 c water
  1 c honey
  Lemon juice to taste

For the pastry: Combine the nuts, sugar, cinnamon and cloves. Place 10–12 sheets of phyllo pastry in a 9"x13" pan, brushing every other sheet evenly with the melted butter. Cover unused pastry with a damp cloth. Spread ⅓ of the nut mixture on the buttered top sheet, then another 5–6 sheets of pastry, buttering every other sheet. Sprinkle another ⅓ of nut mixture over top sheet, then 5–6 more sheets and the final ⅓ of mixture. Spread the remaining pastry sheets on top, buttering every other sheet. With a sharp knife, cut baklava into diamond-shaped pieces. Heat the remaining butter, about ½ c, until very hot and beginning to brown. Pour evenly over the pastry. Sprinkle with a few drops of cold water, then bake at 350° for 30 minutes. Reduce temperature to 300° and continue to bake for 1 hour. Cool, then pour hot syrup over the baklava.

For the syrup: Combine the sugar and water and bring to a boil. Continue boiling for 15 minutes or until syrup is slightly thick. Add honey and bring to boiling point again. Add lemon juice to taste.

Makes 30–36 servings.

Cleo E. Blackstone,
Administrative Staff

Kulachi

Nut Bread Rolls

Rolls:
½ lb butter, melted
5 egg yolks
5 tbsp sugar
1 c sour cream
1 pkg dry yeast
4 c flour

Filling:
5 egg whites
4 c ground nuts
½ lb butter, melted
1 c sugar
1 tsp vanilla

For the rolls: Mix together the egg yolks and sugar, then add the sour cream and yeast. Mix these ingredients with the butter, then the flour. Divide the dough into 4 parts. Roll each section to ½" thick and place on waxed paper.

For the filling: Beat the egg whites until stiff. Add the nuts, melted butter, sugar, and vanilla. Spread the filling equally on the 4 rolls. Roll each like a jelly roll and place on a large cookie sheet with rolled sides touching. Bake at 325° for 45–50 minutes.

Carol (Mrs. Don) James,
Coaching Staff

Peanut Butter Fudge

2 c packed light brown sugar
1 c granulated sugar
1 c light cream or evaporated
  milk
1 tbsp butter or margarine

1 tsp vanilla extract
2–3 tbsp peanut butter
½ c chopped pecans or
  walnuts

In a 3-qt saucepan, cook the sugars and cream over low heat, stirring constantly with a wooden spoon, until the sugar dissolves and the mixture comes to a boil. Cook, stirring occasionally, until the mixture reaches 238° on a candy thermometer, or a little dropped in cold water forms a soft ball. Remove from heat and add the butter. Set aside and cool to lukewarm, about 110°. Add the vanilla and peanut butter, then beat the mixture with a wooden spoon until thick and creamy. Stir in the nuts. Quickly spread in a buttered 9" x 9" pan, covered with buttered waxed paper. Let the candy cool completely, then refrigerate. Remove from the pan in 1 piece and peel off the waxed paper. Cut into pieces.

Makes 1½ lb.

Joyce Johnson,
Tyee

Buckeyes

Chocolate-Covered Peanut Butter Candy

1 (18-oz) jar peanut butter
1 tsp vanilla
1 (1-lb) box powdered sugar

1 (12-oz) pkg chocolate chips
½ cake paraffin

Cream together the peanut butter, vanilla and powdered sugar. Mix well and form into ¾" balls. In a double boiler, melt together the chocolate chips and paraffin. Using a toothpick, dip the balls into the chocolate, coating ¾ of each ball. Reheat the chocolate if it begins to thicken. After the chocolate dipping, dip each ball into ice water. Set balls on waxed paper. Smooth over the hole from the toothpick.

Makes 75.

Kathy Seba,
Athlete

Double Peanut Clusters

½ c peanut butter   1 c whole salted peanuts
1 c semisweet chocolate chips

Combine the peanut butter and chocolate chips in a double boiler
and cook until the chocolate melts. Stir until blended, then add the
peanuts. Stir until the peanuts are well coated. Drip by teaspoonful
onto waxed-paper-lined baking sheets. Chill until set.

Makes 2 dozen.   Alan Erickson,
                                                         Athlete

Peanut Butter-Filled Candy

⅓ c butter or margarine   2 tsp rum flavoring
⅓ c light corn syrup   1 tsp grated orange peel
1 (1-lb) box confectioners'   1 c peanut butter
  sugar   ¼ c honey

Combine the butter, corn syrup, sugar, rum flavoring and orange
peel. Stir until mixture cleans the bowl. Knead until the mixture
forms a smooth ball. Roll out on waxed paper into an 11" x 17" rectangle. Mix the peanut butter and honey. Spread the mixture quickly
over the rectangle. Roll up from the long side. Wrap the roll and chill
until hard. Cut into ½" slices. Chill until ready to serve.

Makes 1 roll, 17" long.   Sue Broome,
                                                         Athlete

Gridiron Brownies from Aunt Alma

Brownies:
4 sq Baker's unsweetened
  chocolate
½ c butter or margarine
2 c granulated sugar
4 eggs
1 c flour
½ tsp baking powder
½ tsp salt
2 tsp vanilla
1 c chopped walnuts

Frosting:
½ c margarine
3 sq Baker's unsweetened
  chocolate
4 c powdered sugar,
  sifted
1 tsp vanilla
1 egg yolk
Milk or half-and-half

For the brownies: Melt the chocolate and butter over low heat in a double boiler. Pour the melted mixture into a separate bowl and beat in the sugar. Add the eggs, one at a time, beating thoroughly after each is added. Slowly add the flour, baking powder and salt, then the vanilla. Stir in the nuts. Pour the mixture into a greased and floured 9" x 13" pan. Bake in a preheated 350° oven for 30 minutes.

For the frosting: Melt the margarine and chocolate in a double boiler over low heat. Pour this mixture into a separate bowl and add the sugar, vanilla and egg yolk. Add a little milk or half-and-half to obtain the proper consistency for spreading. Let the brownies cool for 30 minutes before frosting.

Steve Potter,
Sports Editor

Rich Chocolate Caramels

1 c granulated sugar
1 c packed brown sugar
½ c corn syrup
½ c half-and-half
2 sq unsweetened chocolate

2 tbsp butter or margarine, cut
  in pieces
1 tsp vanilla
25 almonds or pecan halves

Place the sugars, corn syrup, half-and-half and chocolate in a large, heavy saucepan. Heat until the chocolate is melted and the sugars are dissolved. On medium heat, continue cooking the mixture, stirring occasionally, until it reaches 248° on a candy thermometer, or a little dropped in cold water forms a firm ball. Remove the mixture from the heat and quickly stir in the butter and vanilla until thoroughly blended. Pour the mixture into a greased 8" x 8" pan. Cool, then cut in small squares. Top each square with a nut and wrap individually in plastic or foil. Store in a cool, dry place.

Makes 1½ lb.

Steve Jackson,
Athlete

Date Roll

3 c sugar
1 c evaporated milk
3 tbsp margarine
3 tbsp light corn syrup

1 c chopped dates
1 c chopped walnuts
1 tsp vanilla

Combine the sugar, milk, margarine and corn syrup in a saucepan. Bring the mixture to a boil, stirring constantly. Add the dates, then boil the mixture until it reaches 238° on a candy thermometer, or a little dropped in cold water forms a soft ball. Remove from the heat and add the walnuts and vanilla. Beat until thick, then place the mixture on a board. Shape it into 2 rolls, about 1¾" in diameter, and wrap them in waxed paper. Refrigerate, then slice into ⅓" thick pieces to serve.

Makes 2¼ lb.

Steve Burks,
Athlete

Chocolate Granny Bars

⅓ c butter
3 c granola
1 c semisweet chocolate chips
½ c coconut

½ c slivered almonds
1 (14-oz) can sweetened
 condensed milk

Melt the butter in a 9" x 13" pan in the oven. Rotate the pan so that the butter covers the bottom. Slightly crush the granola and sprinkle evenly over the butter. Bake at 325° for 15 minutes. Sprinkle the chocolate chips, coconut and almonds over the granola. Drizzle the condensed milk evenly over the top. Bake at 325° for 20 minutes, or until lightly browned. While still warm, run a knife around the edges to loosen. When cool, cut into bars.

Flossie (Mrs. Don) Smith,
Administrative Staff

Almond Squares

These crunchy cookies are similar to the familiar Italian biscotti.

1 c flour
¾ c ground almonds
¾ c powdered sugar
½ c butter, room temperature
¼ c egg whites
2 oz unsweetened chocolate,
 grated

2 oz semisweet chocolate,
 grated
1 egg, lightly beaten
20 blanched whole almonds

Combine the flour, ground almonds, sugar, butter, egg whites and both chocolates in a bowl and blend thoroughly. Pour mixture into a greased 8"x 8" pan, spreading evenly to the edges. Brush the top with the beaten egg. Mark into squares and top each with a whole almond. Bake at 350° for 35–40 minutes.

Makes 16.

Jeff Partridge,
Athlete

Wheat Germ Brownies

6 tbsp butter
1½ c wheat germ
½ c flour
1 tsp baking powder
1 tsp baking soda
¼ c sugar

1 egg
¾ c dried milk
¼ c molasses
¾ c chopped walnuts
¾ c raisins

Melt the butter. Sift together the wheat germ, flour, baking powder and baking soda. Add the sugar, egg, milk, molasses, walnuts and raisins, then the melted butter. Press mixture into a 9" x 9" pan. Bake at 375° for 12–15 minutes.

John N. Lein,
Member of the Cabinet

Korynne's Buttermilk Brownies

Brownies:
2 c sugar
2 c flour
1 tsp baking soda
1 c margarine
1 c water
4 tbsp cocoa
2 eggs
½ c buttermilk
1 tsp vanilla

Frosting:
½ c margarine
4 tbsp cocoa
1 tbsp buttermilk
1 (1-lb) box powdered sugar
1 c nuts
1 tsp vanilla

For the brownies: Sift together the sugar, flour and soda. Bring margarine, water and cocoa to a boil and pour over the dry ingredients. Add the eggs, buttermilk and vanilla and beat well. Bake at 350° in a large foil-lined pan for 35 minutes, or in a jelly-roll pan for 20 minutes. Frost the brownies while warm.

For the frosting: Bring the margarine, cocoa and buttermilk to a boil. Add the sugar, nuts and vanilla and beat well. Pour over the brownies.

Karen Halverson,
Washington Student
Athletic Board

Ice-Box Cookies

From my grandmother's recipe box.

1 c chopped nuts
1 c white sugar
1 c brown sugar
3 eggs, well beaten
4 c flour

1 c melted fat
1 tsp salt
1 tsp baking soda
1 tsp baking powder

Mix all the ingredients thoroughly and form into 2 rolls, 2" in diameter and 14" in length. Let stand in refrigerator overnight. Slice the rolls into thin pieces and bake on a floured baking sheet at 350° for 10–12 minutes, or until lightly browned.

Makes 4 dozen.

Rena Lude,
Administrative Staff

Apricot Pinwheels

Filling:
1 (8-oz) pkg dried apricots,
    finely chopped
½ c sugar
½ c water
¼ c chopped walnuts or
    pecans

Dough:
2 c unsifted flour
½ tsp salt
½ tsp baking soda
½ c butter or margarine,
    softened
1 c sugar
1 egg
½ tsp vanilla

For the filling: In a small saucepan, combine the apricots, sugar and water. Cook, stirring constantly, for 5 minutes or until thickened. Remove from heat, stir in the nuts and let the mixture cool completely.

For the dough: Sift the flour with the salt and baking soda. In a small mixing bowl, beat the butter, sugar, egg and vanilla until light and fluffy. At low speed, beat in the sifted ingredients until just combined. Divide the dough into 4 parts. Roll out, 1 part at a time, between 2 sheets of waxed paper, to form 8" x 6" rectangles. Spread each rectangle with ¼ of the filling. From the wide end, roll the rectangles tightly, then wrap each in waxed paper. Refrigerate for 2 hours or until firm. Slice the rolls in ¼" pieces and arrange them 1" apart, on greased baking sheets. Bake at 375° for 6 minutes or until lightly browned.

Makes 8 dozen.

Warren de Lisle,
Athlete

Butterscotch Chocolate Chip Bars

1 c shortening
3¾ c brown sugar
6 eggs
4 c flour, unsifted

3¾ tsp baking powder
¾ tsp salt
1½ c chocolate chips
1½ c chopped nuts

Cream together the shortening, brown sugar and eggs. Sift together the flour, baking powder and salt; add to the shortening mixture. Mix in the chocolate chips and nuts. Place in 2 (9" x 13") pans lined with waxed paper. Bake at 350° for 30–35 minutes.

Sue Kruszewski,
Coaching Staff

Grandma's Gingerbread Cookies

This is a wonderful cookie for small children to make. The dough becomes more pliable with handling, never sticks to the board and makes good-tasting cookies.

1 c molasses	1½ tsp ginger
½ c shortening	1 tsp salt
2½ c sifted all-purpose flour	1 tsp cinnamon
2 tsp baking soda	

Heat the molasses until little bubbles form at the edges. Add the shortening and stir until melted. Remove from heat. Sift the dry ingredients together and stir into the molasses mixture, mixing well. Chill the dough for 2 hours. Roll out dough as thin as possible (¼" or less) on a lightly floured board and cut with a cookie cutter. Place on an ungreased baking sheet and bake at 350° for 8–10 minutes. Remove cookies from the sheets immediately after removal from the oven.

Makes 4 dozen.

Mereda (Mrs. W.W.) Metz,
Tyee

Jeni's Chocolate Chip Cookies

2 c Crisco	2 tsp baking soda
2 c white sugar	1 tbsp baking powder
2 c brown sugar	4 c oatmeal
4 eggs	1 large bag chocolate chips
4 c flour	4 tsp vanilla
2 tsp salt	Chopped nuts (optional)

Cream the Crisco and the sugars. Blend in the eggs. Add the flour, salt, soda and baking powder and mix thoroughly. Stir in the oatmeal and chocolate chips, and the nuts if desired. Add the vanilla. Drop from a teaspoon onto a greased cookie sheet. Bake at 350° for 8–10 minutes.

Makes 6 dozen.

Carol James,
Coaching Staff

Chocolate Chip Cookies

2¼ c all-purpose flour
1 tsp baking soda
½ tsp salt
½ c margarine
½ c shortening
¾ c granulated sugar
¾ c brown sugar

2 eggs
1 tsp vanilla
1 c All-Bran or Bran Buds cereal
1 pkg semisweet chocolate chips

Stir together the flour, soda and salt. Cream the margarine, shortening, granulated sugar and brown sugar until will blended. Beat in the eggs and vanilla. Mix in the dry ingredients, then add the cereal and chocolate chips. Drop by the teaspoonful onto greased baking sheets. Bake at 350° for 10–12 minutes, or until lightly browned. Remove from the baking sheets and cool on racks.

Makes 5 dozen.

Paul Coty,
Athlete

Sesame Seed Cookies

1 c butter
1 c sugar
1 egg, beaten
1 tsp vanilla

2 c flour
½ tsp baking soda
¼ tsp salt
1 c toasted sesame seeds

Cream the butter and sugar, then mix in the egg and vanilla. Sift the flour with the baking soda and salt; stir into the creamed mixture. Chill for 1 hour. Form the dough into small balls and roll them in the sesame seeds. Place on greased baking sheets and flatten with the bottom of a glass. Bake at 375° for 10–12 minutes.

Makes 10 dozen.

Clifton Johnson,
Athlete

Homemade Oatmeal Cookie Mix

Mix:
2½ c all-purpose flour
2 tsp salt
1 tsp soda
2 c firmly-packed brown
  sugar
1 c granulated sugar
1½ c shortening

6 cups quick or old-fashioned
  oats, uncooked

Cookies:
3⅓ c cookie mix
1 egg
3 tbsp water
1 tsp vanilla

For the mix: In a large bowl, mix the flour, salt and soda. Add the sugars and mix well. Cut in the shortening until well blended, then stir in the oats. Store the mix in a tightly-covered container in the refrigerator or a cool, dry place for up to 3 months. (Makes 13⅓ c mix.)

For the cookies: In a medium bowl, combine all the ingredients. Mix with a spoon or fork until a stiff dough forms, about 1 minute. Drop by rounded teaspoonfuls onto a greased baking sheet. Bake in a preheated 350° oven for 15 minutes or until golden brown.

Variations: For Raisin-Spice Cookies, add ½ c raisins, ½ tsp cinnamon, ¼ tsp nutmeg and ⅛ tsp cloves to a batch of mix. For Oatmeal Chippers, add ½ c semisweet chocolate chips. For Sunny Nut Drops, add ½ c chopped nuts and 1 tsp grated lemon or orange peel.

Makes 3 dozen.

Jacquie Brown,
Tyee

Grandma's Old-Fashioned Oatmeal Cookies

1½ c sifted flour
½ tsp baking soda
2 tsp cinnamon
1 tsp allspice
1 tsp nutmeg
½ tsp cloves
1 tsp salt

½ c butter
1½ c sugar
1 egg, well beaten
3 ripe bananas, mashed
2 c quick-cooking oatmeal
1 c chopped nuts
1 c chocolate chips

Sift together the flour, soda, spices and salt. Cream the butter with the sugar until fluffy. Add the eggs and the bananas, mixing well. Stir in the flour mixture, then the oats, nuts and chocolate chips. Let the batter stand for 10 minutes. Drop from a teaspoon onto a greased baking sheet. Bake at 375° for 10–12 minutes.

Makes 40 cookies.

Yvette Lewis,
Athlete

Oatmeal Cookies

3 eggs, well beaten
1 c raisins
1 tsp vanilla
1 c shortening
1 c brown sugar
1 c granulated sugar

2½ c sifted flour
1 tsp salt
2 tsp baking soda
1 tsp cinnamon
2 c oatmeal
½ c chopped walnuts

Combine the eggs, raisins and vanilla. Let the mixture stand for 1 hour. Thoroughly cream together the shortening and sugars. Sift the flour, salt, soda and cinnamon into the sugar mixture. Mix well. Blend in the eggs and raisins, the oatmeal and the nuts. The dough will be stiff. Drop in heaping teaspoonfuls onto an ungreased baking sheet, or roll into small balls, flatten between hands and place on the sheet. Bake in a preheated 350° oven for 10–12 minutes or until lightly browned. Do not overbake.

Rena Lude,
Administrative Staff

Old-Fashioned Chocolate Ice Cream

2 pkg unflavored gelatin
½ c cold water
1 c milk
¾ c sugar
1 (1-lb) can Hershey's
   chocolate syrup

2 c light cream
2 c heavy cream
2 tbsp vanilla

Soften the gelatin in the cold water for 5 minutes in a saucepan. Add the milk and sugar. Cook the mixture over medium heat, stirring constantly, until the gelatin and sugar are dissolved. Remove from heat and add the chocolate syrup. Cool for 10 minutes. Add the light cream, heavy cream and vanilla. Freeze in an ice cream freezer according to manufacturer's directions.

Makes 2 qt.

Carlin McClary,
Athlete

Chocolate Almond Ice Cream

⅔ c chocolate syrup
⅔ c sweetened condensed
   milk
2 c whipping cream

½ tsp vanilla
⅓ c chopped almonds,
   toasted

In a mixing bowl, combine the chocolate syrup, condensed milk, cream and vanilla. Chill until very cold, then whip until the mixture forms fluffy soft peaks. Fold in the nuts. Pile the mixture in a refrigerator tray. Freeze until firm. Serve with toasted almonds sprinkled on top.

Serves 6–8.

Betty Ryan,
Member of the Cabinet

Southern Peach Ice Cream

4 lb peaches	1 pt heavy cream
Juice of 2 lemons	1 c half-and-half
1 tsp almond flavoring	2½ c sugar

Wash, peel, pit and cut the peaches into chunks. Place the pieces in a blender and whirl until puréed. Pour into a large bowl and add the lemon juice, almond flavoring, cream, half-and-half and sugar. Pour the mixture into the can of an ice cream freezer and freeze according to manufacturer's directions.

Makes 4 qt.

Dr. Harvey Cross,
Faculty Representative

Coach Stull's Pumpkin Cookies with Penuche Frosting

Cookies:
1 c butter
½ c firmly-packed brown
  sugar
½ c granulated sugar
1 c canned pumpkin
1 egg
1 tsp vanilla
2 c flour
1 tsp baking soda

1 tsp baking powder
1 tsp cinnamon
½ tsp salt
1 c chopped nuts

Frosting:
3 tbsp butter
½ c brown sugar
¼ c milk
2 c powdered sugar

For the cookies: Cream the butter and sugars together; add the pumpkin, egg and vanilla, mixing well. Add the sifted dry ingredients and blend well. Add the nuts. Drop from a teaspoon onto an ungreased baking sheet. Bake at 350° for 10–12 minutes. Cool.

For the frosting: Combine the butter and brown sugar in a saucepan; bring to a boil. Cook and stir 1 minute or until slightly thickened. Cool about 15 minutes. Add milk and beat until smooth. Add enough powdered sugar for spreading consistency.

Makes 6½ dozen.

Kim Stull,
Coaching Staff

Apricot Cheese Pillows

8 prepared crêpes
6 tbsp slivered almonds
2 tbsp butter

Filling:
1 (8-oz) pkg cream cheese,
  room temperature
¼ c butter, room temperature
¼ c sugar

1½ tsp vanilla
1 tsp grated lemon rind

Sauce:
⅔ c apricot jam
⅓ c orange juice
2 tbsp butter
1 tbsp lemon juice
1½ tsp grated lemon rind

In a small mixing bowl, combine all the ingredients for the filling and beat on low speed until fluffy. Spread each crêpe almost to the edge with 3 tbsp cheese filling. Fold envelope style. Arrange the filled crêpes in a buttered shallow dish and dot with butter. Bake in a 350° oven for 10 minutes or until cheese is bubbling. Remove the crêpes to a serving platter, top with apricot sauce and sprinkle with the slivered almonds.

For the sauce: Combine all the sauce ingredients in a saucepan. Place over low heat and stir until smooth.

Serves 8.

Jeanne Calderhead,
Tyee

Peach Crisp

Delicious served either warm or cold with cream.

8 ripe peaches   ½ c sugar
¼ tsp cinnamon   Pinch of salt
½ c sifted flour   ¼ c butter or margarine

Peel, pit and slice the peaches. Place them in the bottom of a greased 1-qt baking dish and sprinkle with cinnamon. Sift the flour, sugar and salt into a mixing bowl. Cut in the butter or margarine until the mixture is mealy. Spoon the mixture over the peaches. Bake at 450° for 15 minutes; then reduce the oven temperature to 375° and continue baking for 20–25 minutes, until the top is crisp.

Serves 4.   Paul Coty,
                                             Athlete

Hot Chocolate Mix

This mix adapts to dorm life very well. It doesn't require refrigeration, is quick to make and leaves no mess. Soothing for the night-before-the-big-game jitters.

1 (8-qt) box dry Carnation
  milk
1 (1-lb) box Nestlé's Quick

½ c powdered sugar
1 (6-oz) jar Coffee Mate

Mix all the ingredients together and store in an air-tight container. To serve, fill a cup ⅓ full with dry mixture, then fill with boiling water. Stir and enjoy.

Chris O'Connor,
Athlete

INDEX

INDEX

Soups

Salads

Casseroles & Sandwiches

INDEX

Desserts & Sweets

Order Form

Please send me ☐ cookbooks at $8.95, plus $1.25 per book postage and handling.

Name _____

Address _____

City _____ State _____ Zip _____

Total number of books _____ Total enclosed _____
Charge to: _____
VISA # _____ Exp. date _____
MasterCard # _____ Exp. date _____

Send order to: Sports Information Office
                  Graves Building
                  University of Washington
                  Seattle, WA   98105

- -

Order Form

Please send me ☐ cookbooks at $8.95, plus $1.25 per book postage and handling.

Name _____

Address _____

City _____ State _____ Zip _____

Total number of books _____ Total enclosed _____
Charge to: _____
VISA # _____ Exp. date _____
MasterCard # _____ Exp. date _____

Send order to: Sports Information Office
                  Graves Building
                  University of Washington
                  Seattle, WA   98105